Please Excuse My Daughter

Please Excuse My Daughter

JULIE KLAM

RIVERHEAD BOOKS
a member of Penguin Group (USA) Inc.
New York
2008

RIVERHEAD BOOKS
Published by the Penguin Group
Penguin Group (USA) Inc., 375 Hudson Street, New York, New York 10014, USA • Penguin Group (Canada), 90 Eglinton Avenue East, Suite 700, Toronto, Ontario M4P 2Y3, Canada (a division of Pearson Penguin Canada Inc.) • Penguin Books Ltd, 80 Strand, London WC2R 0RL, England • Penguin Ireland, 25 St Stephen's Green, Dublin 2, Ireland (a division of Penguin Books Ltd) • Penguin Group (Australia), 250 Camberwell Road, Camberwell, Victoria 3124, Australia (a division of Pearson Australia Group Pty Ltd) • Penguin Books India Pvt Ltd, 11 Community Centre, Panchsheel Park, New Delhi–110 017, India • Penguin Group (NZ), 67 Apollo Drive, Rosedale, North Shore 0632, New Zealand (a division of Pearson New Zealand Ltd) • Penguin Books (South Africa) (Pty) Ltd, 24 Sturdee Avenue, Rosebank, Johannesburg 2196, South Africa

Penguin Books Ltd, Registered Offices:
80 Strand, London WC2R 0RL, England

A portion of this work was originally published in different form in *Glamour.*

Published simultaneously in Canada

Library of Congress Cataloging-in-Publication Data

Klam, Julie.
Please excuse my daughter / Julie Klam.
p. cm.
ISBN 978-1-59448-980-8
1. Klam, Julie. 2. Authors, American—21st century—Biography. I. Title.
PS3611.L35Z465 2008 2007035968
813'.6—dc22
[B]

Printed in the United States of America
1 3 5 7 9 10 8 6 4 2

Book design by Amanda Dewey

For my mother

and

for my daughter

But take utmost care and watch yourselves scrupulously, so that you do not forget the things that you saw with your own eyes and so that they do not fade from your mind as long as you live. And make them known to your children and to your children's children.

—DEUTERONOMY 4:9

You know what made *Angela's Ashes* such a wonderful book? Frank McCourt didn't judge. He just told the story. He didn't say his mother and father were bad people; he just told what they did and let the readers decide for themselves. You understand? They weren't bad. They didn't do anything wrong on purpose. It's just how it was.

—MY MOTHER 7:45

Please Excuse My Daughter

One

Early Retirement

ON FEBRUARY 13, 1997, I was thirty years old, 35,000 feet in the air, and very seriously contemplating retirement. As I headed to Florida, sitting there in the clouds, eating my tiny Florentine omelet and listening to Peter Allen's "Fly Away" on SkyTunes, the only argument against retiring that I could come up with was that no one would really notice; retirement would be barely distinguishable from the life I was already leading.

The previous June I'd quit my job as a death claims clerk at my father's insurance and financial-planning firm to try writing full-time. I had been doing both for six years and felt like I was getting too comfortable in my appropriate office attire.

My best friend, Jancee, an editor at *Rolling Stone* magazine at the time, got glassy-eyed when I told her over a cramped lunch in her cubicle. "You are so lucky," she moaned. "You're going to get to watch *Oprah*."

"Uh, not exactly," I snapped. "I'm going to be *working*, just like you, except my commute will be shorter."

"What I would do to wear my sweatpants all day," she swooned. "And the first thing I would do would be to stop wearing a bra, except for public appearances."

"Yeah, that is exactly my motive," I said. "Once again, you've crystallized my thoughts completely."

I started my freelance career with a strict schedule of writing, pitching magazine stories, diligently following up, no daytime TV, no shopping lunches with my mother. In a matter of a few months, the plan began to erode. I was a person with little experience, less confidence, and a complete inability to handle rejection. It was a bad combination for a writer. My job was to be a salesman of myself, except as far as I was concerned, the product was a lemon.

At the time, most people still didn't use e-mail, so pitches had to be sent by mail and followed up by phone. Instead of just being ignored (which is not great, but not actively painful) you had to actually hear the lack of enthusiasm in a person's voice while you talked. I loathed it. When an editor was snotty or unresponsive to me, I'd stop pitching altogether for weeks.

My gung-ho attitude quickly dissolved and my daily routine slowly devolved into hour-long phone calls with my mother and hanging out with my aunt Mattie. The Upper

East Side apartment Mattie shared with her husband, Dave, and dog, Harry, became a second home to me and my dog, Otto.

These visits were my postgraduate studies or finishing school. Otto, a Boston terrier I had rescued from the cheesesteak-scrapped streets of Philadelphia, and I would walk over from my Upper West Side apartment and sit at Mattie's dining room table. She was a painter and a lyricist who took care of me: advising me, feeding me, and shoving twenty-dollar bills into my pocket when I headed to the elevator. I was able to hide from the harsh world but stick to a comforting schedule: playing cards, snacking, watching daytime TV (*Judge Judy*, *Jerry Springer*—never something as respectable as *Oprah*), and reading the tabloids. I would amuse myself by walking into her apartment on Friday after a full week of slacking and shrieking, "TGIF!"

The fact that I wasn't earning any money interfered with nothing. Certainly not my wardrobe. If there's one thing my mother has always been game for, it's buying outfits for potential situations. The mere mention of an editor or a meeting sends my mother flying to the nearest outlets. Overnight a package arrives with fabulous ensembles for any time of day or year. I've always felt sorry for my clothing, which sits in my closet, so hopeful, so disappointed.

"I'm going to be in a jacket photo of the author!" spouts the TSE black cashmere sweater reduced from $750 to $450.

"Don't get too excited. I thought I was going to L.A. for a meeting with Goldie Hawn," replies the Ralph Lauren seersucker suit. *"That was over a year ago. I still have my tags on."*

"Please! You're timeless! How many years do I have to wait for a splashy party?" cries the aqua beaded and sequined Lotta halter top. *"I could've belonged to Jessica Simpson! I could've gone down the red carpet!"*

Once again, I had packed a bag without any of them, hearing their sighs as I closed the closet door, taking just a shredded cargo miniskirt and tank tops and, of course, sweatpants. I was heading to Florida—vacationland, even though I was the last person who'd be needing some R&R.

The trip to Florida was recreational only in part. I was meeting my older brother Matt, who was coming from D.C. We were there to give comfort and support to my mother's father, Grandpa Saul. My grandmother Pearl had recently passed away, and each member of the family, his four daughters and their eleven children, took turns visiting. He was trying to sort out his life and figure out who he was without my grandmother, his wife of sixty-three years, to define him.

From the minute we stepped off our respective planes, we were in Geezerville. Grandpa Saul couldn't meet us at the airport. He sent one of his retirement-community cronies whom we'd encountered many times before. His name was something like, but not, Hy Heisenmount, though that's exactly what Matt and I called him, because we liked it better. Hy was a formerly wealthy and currently destitute senior, robbed blind by an unscrupulous business manager. Now, in order to survive, he had to chauffeur other people's grandkids to and from the airport for cash. A series of humiliating rides into his sunset years. He had a constipated face, personality, and voice. He always got especially rattled by the checking of luggage, so of course Matt had decided to check his tiny carry-on bag.

"Uhn, you checked, uhn?" Hy grunted.

"Yes," Matt declared, "I checked."

"Oy." Hy was unable to hide his disappointment. "You see, the problem with checking is it can add so much time to the trip, potentially getting you caught up in rush hour. Also it could get lost or misplaced."

Then finally the truth came out.

"I have a dinner appointment at five o'clock in Delray," Hy sighed.

It was eleven a.m. He'd have approximately six hours to travel twenty minutes. In Florida, this is known as "cutting it close." He used his "car phone" to call his wife and alert her to the luggage debacle.

When we arrived at my grandfather's house, I felt all of my stresses ebb. In a way, it was like going to sleep. You had nothing to do but be there. He lived in a gated retirement community in South Florida called Woodmont, a neat little world where every house looked the same, with slight variations in landscaping. His was on Pine Circle, which intersected with Pine Street, Pine Lane, and Pine Drive. I so wanted to be part of that coniferous world composed of former New York/New Jersey Jewish senior citizens who ate dinner at four-thirty, yelled at waiters, and took the remains of the breadbasket home in their handbags because "it was illegal to serve again." There were no unknowns in Woodmont. You lived in your little white house with palm trees that were lit with blue and green and red at night. The lawns were like plush carpet, the street softly paved. You had an air-conditioned house, a garage, a car, a clubhouse, and challah from Publix. There were no bugs (or any nonhuman life forms, for that matter) because, as my dad said, "They sprayed the shit out of the place."

My grandfather greeted us with tears in his eyes and a hug that didn't end. He was bald with a mustache, a dead ringer for Philippe Noiret, who played Pablo Neruda in *Il Postino*, except he wore lime-green Sansabelts from Jacks for Slacks. He was elegantly groomed, with even his nails manicured.

Already antsy, Matt went for a run. He detested this antiseptic bubble world that I loved. Matt, a fiction writer, was the anti-me, a world traveler and voracious experiencer of life, who loved T-shirts with slogans on them like "Kiss Me, I'm Pro-Choice!" While I spent my life attempting to make people feel good and comfortable, Matt wanted just the opposite. His short stories brought family and friends to tears, because they were raw, barely concealed character sketches of the people he knew, shown at their most vulnerable. I always had the same unpleasant mix of feelings when I read his work: proud and nauseated.

Matt was also more driven than I was, but then again, so was a cat playing with a ball of yarn. The friction in our relationship came from his regular rants about how I should get off my ass. Despite this, we always had a great time together and made each other laugh uncontrollably, and I looked forward to spending this time with him away from the distractions of his dizzying social life.

One of the great oddities of a Florida visit was that our grandparents didn't go outside. If you wanted to be with them, you had to sit inside on their white leather couch while they ate Andes candies and watched *Wheel of Fortune*. Though you came from New York, where the weather was 32 degrees and sleeting, and all everyone in Florida talked about was how great the weather was (80 degrees, sunny, balmy breezes), you couldn't actually experience it firsthand. Each morning my grandfather sat with the paper and told us the weather we were missing, in N.Y., D.C., and, let's be honest, Florida, too.

If we got lucky and he had a card game, then we could go out. We didn't waste a second dashing off to the deserted pool. Well, it wasn't entirely deserted; there was always the guy skimming the one leaf off of it and the woman replacing the unused towels. Maybe it was the extensive list of rules: No long hair, no peeing in the pool, no improper swim attire, no broken glass in the pool, no radios, no floats, no splashing, no diving, no horseplay, no laughing, no joy, no, no, NO! The ideal Woodmont pool user would be a sterile, hairless individual who would walk down the steps, slowly dip his body into the water, careful not to dislodge any skin particles, then just as carefully step out of the pool and remove his dripping body from the premises.

Matt made it his business to break every rule, first jumping in the pool fully clothed with his shoes on. Improper pool attire, check. I watched a cloud of yellow follow him.

"What are you, five? Are you peeing in the pool?" I asked.

"Yep." He backstroked, shaking his shoulder-length hair in the direction of the pump and singing "Rebel, Rebel."

I envied him. He was so sure of himself and so not concerned with anyone else's opinion. He came out of the pool, stripped down to his bathing trunks, and, dragging a chaise longue across the tiles (another no-no), lotioned up and lay down directly on the chair, no towel to keep it from getting sticky. He was like the Che Guevara of the pool area.

"So what have you been doing?" An innocuous-enough question from someone else, someone who wasn't my big, bossy older brother.

"I just did a Q&A with K. D. Lang for *Rolling Stone*'s Women in Rock issue," I said.

He shook water from his ear and asked, "Did you kiss her?" once again trying to make me uncomfortable.

"It was on the phone."

"So what else are you doing?" he demanded.

"I'm pitching a bunch of stuff," I said.

Any call to Jancee constituted a pitch meeting in my mind. Jancee and I were both writers, but she had an ambition and fearlessness and drive that I could not hope to match. I had a tentative, halfhearted uncertainty and a fear of getting to bed after nine p.m. When Jancee had an assignment for me she would preface it with "It might be late, but you can wear your pajamas to the show." I'd go interview Jon Bon Jovi or Simon Le Bon or Bono with an oversized L.L. Bean field coat covering my sweats and "I ❤ My Boston Terrier" T-shirt. I'd get my quotes, leap in a cab, and race home to my three best friends—my bed, my pillow, and my dog. In my defense, I was reliable and always did good work. If Jancee assigned me a piece on Monday that was due Friday it would be on her desk Tuesday, and it would be tight and snappy, and if the word count was 250 words, it would be 250 words, not 249, not 251. I was low maintenance except for the extra time Jancee had to spend praising my every move, from the route I took to the interview to my choice of adjectives. In the same vein as working for my dad, it was always easier for me to have a boss who loved me. And Jancee also knew my limitations; I appreciated her not offering me things that would give me too much anxiety.

Matt was not so concerned with my mental *meshugaas*.

"You know what you should pitch?" Matt said to me. I immediately tuned him out. This was the type of back-and-forth we'd been having our whole lives.

"Call Blah Blah at *Esquire* and Hoo Ha at *Details* and J.J. at *GQ*. Tell them you're my sister and see what they're looking for . . . [*tune out*]. Make a list of every new trend [*tune out*], every editor in the city . . . [*tune out*] fact-checking jobs . . . [*tune out*] copy editing . . . [*tune out*]. If you really want to write . . . [*tune out*] editorial assistant." My ethos of doing as little as I could get away with drove Matt insane, so he figured he would lecture me with a baseball bat. I nodded, the compliant dead horse. "Sounds good, dude. Thanks!"

By then it was time to meet Grandpa at the clubhouse for his usual budget lunch—a soup-wich (cup of soup, half a sandwich). It would be ordered, eaten, and paid for in under ten minutes and Grandpa would return to his cards, sending us back to the pool.

At around 3:45 my anxiety-ridden grandfather would come to collect us, already dressed for dinner in his Grandpa Look—white sports jacket, pink-and-white-plaid pants, white loafers, pink shirt. He stood by the edge of the pool, wondering aloud if we would be leaving ourselves enough time to shower and get changed. The most hideous crime imaginable to a Florida senior is to miss the Early Bird dinner. Missing the dinner can turn the joyous occasion of eating the equivalent of Amtrak food in a loud dining hall into something even worse: overpaying for that experience. We'd all sit down at 4:45 and be sipping post-dessert coffee by 5:05, a variety of doggie bags in our possession. Throughout all of this, I had the same warm, drugged feeling. People walked around in stretch pants and Cobbie Cuddler shoes and ate till they were gonna bust. They didn't exercise or count calories or do anything that didn't feel nice. They had earned this place in life, I had not. But I really wanted to skip the middle part where I was going to have to suffer in order to get there.

After dinner, Grandpa and I sat on his front porch, looking at all the Malibu-lit trees while Matt circled the complex on my grandfather's giant tricycle. We talked a lot about life and loss and what comes after. He'd end every conversational thread with "Oh well." And "Yep, yep, yep." And then he'd take his glasses off and clean them. My grandfather had been the caretaker of the whole world as far as I was concerned. He was financially secure and nurturing, provided a million and one safety nets; he was all the clichés the men of his generation embodied—a real gentleman, the last of a dying breed, a class act.

I didn't really get to know him until I was older, and then I found him to be one of the most admirable people I'd ever met. He was whip-smart (he knew every answer on *Jeopardy!* and would phrase them in the form of a question). He was unfailingly generous with his children and grandchildren, paying for medical school, braces, whatever was needed.

I enjoyed a great correspondence with him over the years. While studying silent films at NYU, I'd write and ask him about his memories, then read his responses in class.

> Movies did not play for ten weeks, except possibly in Broadway Theaters, pictures like "The Big Parade" with John Gilbert. "Birth of a Nation" with the Gish Sisters. Admission was five cents, a special picture might go up to ten or eleven cents. My favorite actors were Douglas Fairbanks, The Farnum Brothers, Edmund Lowe. Of course nobody outranked Mary Pickford . . . except maybe Theda Bara. The Silent Era was just as wonderful to us as the present sophisticated pictures. The directors, Erich von Stroheim, Irving Thalberg, C.B. Demille always listed above the stars, you know. Princess, you asked a hell of a lot of questions and my hand is tired. More later! Love.

He also filled me in on what people in America were aware of during World War II, particularly as it concerned the Holocaust.

> Princess, long before WW II began it was already common knowledge the Jews were being annihilated. They knew about the round-up of Jews, the debasement of Jews. They knew about the racial laws—believe me. They knew! They didn't know all about the extent of the horrors of the camps, but they knew they were there, there were actual accounts of the atrocities by people who had suffered them, people who had escaped—by people who paid the Nazis to get out. So we knew. But the governments "didn't know." They closed their eyes. They wouldn't accept immigrants. (Read the book *Ship of Fools.*) This included the U.S., who turned back a shipload of Jews for fear of insulting the German government. These people were eventually sent to prison camps and slaughtered. Read about the Warsaw Ghetto uprising. . . . Anti-Semitism isn't dead. So watch out, kid, take it seriously, it's not a fairy tale. History repeats itself if you don't stop it. Dire predictions? Maybe. Love from the Old Grandpa

In other letters he described the evenings he shared with his friends, dressed in black tie, standing around the piano, singing Ruth Etting, opera, and ragtime. He told me about how when his grandparents came to Ellis Island "the donkeys who were the gods there were too lazy to spell out Coopersmith, so we became the Smiths. Goyim . . ."

About the current state of his life, his feelings were less clear. He had a small group of good friends and a lot of disdain for the rest of the residents. Despite that, he was elected president of his community.

I loved how he refused to get caught up in the petty bullshit that some people fall prey to when they forget who they once were. He handled the ridiculousness of his fellow *alte kaker*s. There was a little bravado and a lot of telling people off: "I told that sonofabitch, 'Take your goddamn letter and shove it up your ass!' "

One night someone knocked on his door, very late, woke him up. It was a woman, with her hair in rollers under a scarf.

"Saul," she said, "as president, I think you should know something." My grandfather braced for the worst. "The C Complex swimming pool has a doody in it."

"What the hell do you want me to do about it?" he barked, then slammed the door on her and returned to bed.

As he told me the story, he got riled up all over again, while I laughed insanely. As I watched Matt rolling by on the giganto-cycle, the thought crossed my mind: Had this incident occurred on one of our visits? Matt certainly would have pooped in the pool if he could have.

"Goddamn imbeciles! They think as president I walk around with some kind of doody-net?"

I suggested that perhaps it had been a come-on. A late-night knock-knock from the seductress in curlers needing rescuing from the poopy in the pool, so very close to her home. A heavy wind might have sent it through her window.

He raised his eyebrows to me, suggesting I might have something there, and then told me that if he did in fact date her, he'd have to get a dolly for her Broward Mall–sized ass.

He was quite fascinated by the fact that his wife's dying had suddenly made him a hot property at Woodmont. Just like that he had his pick of dames in oversized appliquéd wash-and-wear sweaters and knee-highs with Easy Spirits with Aquanetted helmet-dos.

"What about you?" he said and abruptly turned to watch Matt glide around again. I knew what he was thinking, that Matt was going to break the thing. That's what we kids always did, broke stuff.

"What about me?" I asked.

"You have a boyfriend?" he said more directly.

I was not used to my grandfather turning his attention to me in this way. My comfort zone was deeply pierced.

"No boyfriend." I hoped that would end it.

"Let me ask you something: are you a lesbian?"

Jesus Christ, I thought. He and Matt should be talking, not me. I'll ride the trike.

"If only it were that easy," I said, hoping *that* would end it.

"You're thirty. You're not getting any younger. Why don't you just get married and have a family?"

"I don't know how."

"What do you mean?"

I explained how things were nowadays. People were more focused on their careers.

"*You're* not," he said matter-of-factly.

"I'm trying," I said.

"Hmm."

"Women are different, Grandpa. This isn't the 1950s, when you sent your daughters to college to find a rich husband." That sounded good.

"I know all about it. I know lady doctors and lawyers. But you're not a doctor or a lawyer."

"I'm a writer."

End of that conversation. My grandfather had an excellent bullshit detector, and he knew I was at Mattie's every time he called there. I think he just didn't want to go there with me. What was the point? He just sat back and I asked him about his life now.

We talked about how we each spent our days—eerily similar—and that neither of us liked to eat alone in restaurants. I found myself envying him because he didn't really have anything left to figure out. No one expected any more from him.

The morning I was supposed to leave, I asked my grandfather over breakfast if he'd like me to keep him company a while longer. "No," he said, barely looking up from *Brenda Starr* in the *Sun-Sentinel*. "You have to get going." Ouch.

At the airport, Matt made a last-ditch effort to get me to focus.

"You're thirty," he said. I knew that. "You have some thinking to do." Blah, blah, blah, blah, blah, blah, blah . . . I nodded intently every twenty seconds or so. Mercifully, his flight boarded first, and I got to call my mother from a phone booth surrounded by the tiny orange trees that were for sale.

"You're in the airport? Did Matthew leave? Did you have a good time? How was dinner?" My mother needed filling in. I hadn't spoken to her since the previous evening at five p.m., and the call before that in the morning.

"Good, fine," I sighed.

"What? Was somebody mean to you?"

"No. Nobody thinks I'm doing enough. I got about eight million lectures on how empty my life is."

"You're doing the best you can. You'll come back and we'll figure it out. You were going to get a teaching certificate."

I SAT on the return flight to New York, looking much less forward to the swell life that everyone deemed insufficient. I opened my day planner. Blank. I sat back and sighed out the window at the sun's copper reflection on the clouds and my airline headset picked up where I had left it, Peter Allen singing, *"Not today, nobody here is flyin' away-ay . . ."*

NINE DAYS AFTER I got home, my grandfather died. I was back on Pine Circle with the rest of our family. My mother and father and brothers and aunts and uncles and cousins—we were all there. I went into his linen-closet office, where just days earlier he'd showed me the photos he'd covered the walls with, dating back sixty years. I sat down at his white rolltop desk. His correspondence was neatly rubber-banded in a letter holder, there was a cup of sharpened pencils and pens, and small drawers held his checkbook, paper clips, stamps. On the leather-rimmed blotter lay the yellow legal pad, the one he had used to write me letters, the one he had used over the past fourteen years to write his memoir in longhand, which he would mail to my aunt and she would type up.

The top sheet of the pad was filled with his slanted writing.

> I'm writing this as the closing comments after I finish as much of my autobiography as I'm able to. You've all grown up (when I say you, I mean Iris, Phyllis, Marcia, and Mattie [his four daughters]) to be the greatest things that could happen to anyone. I'm so proud of you all that I burst with happiness.
>
> And your children, my grandchildren, Barry, Randy, Stephanie, Laura, Eric, Craig, Jon, Jimmy, Brian, Matthew and Julie—I think that's all of you—have all become people that anyone would be happy to claim as theirs.
>
> And then there's Bernie, Jim, Paul and Dave [his four sons-in-law]. My hat's off to you for being the people you are. I'm also amazed that you have accepted not only the virtues they inherited from their mother (together with the minimal faults that they may have acquired along the way) but also the idea that they are princesses as they're all descended from Royalty (on their mother's side).
>
> I love you all.

What this lovely man left, this note, this legacy, no words could describe. Each member of the family took turns reading the letter and breaking into sobs.

His last words were that I was in fact a princess. And while that notion made me feel adored and cared for, it pointed out even more how ill equipped I was to handle life as an unmarried adult woman. It reminded me of a Halloween I spent in midtown. A woman dressed as Cinderella was trying to get a cab during the taxi-shift turnover.

"Why aren't they stopping?" she asked me.

"They're all off duty," someone said. She had no choice but to join a group of us waiting for the bus.

"Will the driver make change?" she asked, taking a five-dollar bill out of her powder-blue purse, looking around.

"No," a man said, "but you can use my MetroCard."

"Oh, thank you!" she said, tucking the bill back into her purse.

He motioned to it. "Uh, that'll be a dollar fifty, miss."

Cinderella looked surprised.

"I can make the change," the man said.

Princesses pay for mass transit just like everyone else.

When I was a kid, I used to draw elaborate pirate treasure maps. Start where you are, travel over the crocodile canal, through the vampire-bat forest, and end up at the treasure chest clearly marked with a red X. You open the box, brimming with sparkling jewels and gold pieces, slash marks emanating from the box, and you take it to Fifth Avenue to one of the purchasers of estate jewelry and treasure chests and walk away with a briefcase full of money, the end. The letter from my grandfather was like my pirate treasure map, the treasure chest filled with answers. I was now at Start.

Two

Jewish Girls Don't Get Their Hair Wet

WHERE I WAS at thirty had everything to do with the way I grew up, but I wasn't sure exactly how.

I know that kids will choose to emulate one parent or the other. Not necessarily all of the traits; sometimes they choose to handle anger like Mom and stress like Dad. For me the choice was clear. Mom was the princess. She was beautiful, fun, hilarious, happy, and her goal was to give us kids anything we wanted. Bing, bang, boom, she was the popular parent. My dad, on the other hand, got up at dawn to commute to Manhattan, where he stayed till dark. He was either tired or cranky, and he always wanted us to go play outside. As a response to my mother's saying "yippity skippity" to everything, he growled a "no." He was forced to pull the reins in on everything because Mom just wouldn't.

"Dad, can I—"

"No."

"Mom, can—"

"Sure! How much do you need? What colors do you want? How many should I get? When do you want to go?"

It was such a raw deal for my father.

MY MOTHER WOULD DRIVE around my hometown, narrating like some kind of psychotic tour bus guide. Call it Jewish Eye for the Hick Town.

"And to our right is the store with makeup from 1912. They don't need cosmetics here because they are still wearing the same tube of frosty pink shit lipstick that they wore to their debutante ball."

It was 1972 and we'd been living in the village of Katonah in the town of Bedford, New York, for less than two years. I was five and already learning that we were *in* Bedford but not *of* Bedford.

Katonah is a village in northern Westchester County in New York, about forty miles north of midtown Manhattan, where the average house price in 2006 was $912,000 and the average resident wears lime-green pants with blue whales and pink-and-green monogrammed sweaters without a trace of irony.

We stopped at a red light, and my mother coolly critiqued each person crossing the street, like Howard Cosell at a runway show. *"What was she thinking this morning—'I think I'll wear everything brown that I own'? Brown ain't going to cover that ass, honey. You need a tarp."*

I looked at the woman's butt. It was big, but I was five, so all butts were big to me.

"Check this guy out. What is that, a squirrel on his head? [Yelling inside the car.] *YOU'RE FOOLING NO ONE, SIR."*

I was under the tutelage of a master toupee detector; I identified the webbing, the mismatched color, the strange ridge on the back. Yes indeed, this was a piece.

Also covered in this course was nose-job detection, a subtler art but no less vital a life lesson.

"Her plastic surgeon meant to give her the Book of Noses to choose from." She indicated a woman in a seal coat with a fleshy blob of a proboscis. *"But by mistake he gave her the Book of Farm Animals. That's how she ended up with Wilbur's honker,"* she said, referring to the pig in *Charlotte's Web*. I solemnly watched the unknowing freak cross the street, secretly checking my own nose in the rearview mirror.

"Look at this dame. Do you know how much younger she'd look if she'd cover the gray? Do they sell hair dye here? Hey, check in the drugstore next to the dust-covered container of Dippity-Do." Her pitch would rise. *"God. What is wrong with these people? Who is their role model—Methuselah?"*

IN THE EARLY SEVENTIES my mother had straightened, waist-length hair, faux-pony-skin hip-huggers, false eyelashes, and long, manicured nails. She was exotic, and all of my friends said she looked just like Cher. She didn't fit in, nor did she want to. I remember watching her walk through the town while the guy at the bank, the butcher, the gas station owner all leered at her like characters in those old Tex Avery cartoons whose eyes pop out of their heads, tongues lag on the ground, and you hear the AH-OOHGA sound when the tarted-up bunny goes by. Everyone flirted with her, and it was some of the only fun she got to have. She was lonely, and that's where I came in, her conveniently packaged built-in friend. Watching her muck out our horse stalls in the mornings, I had the sense that she felt duped. The princess locked in the manure-strewn glass tower.

Mom had various escapes. She talked on the phone endlessly to her mother and sisters. Each morning the phone would ring four times. My mother's refined speech would dissolve into La Bronx Bomber. She called her mother "Ma" and told her sisters, one after the other, about what a fuckin' nightmeah Yorkshire pudding had been to make.

Like the other women of her generation, she learned to cook from Julia Child, not her own mother. Grandma Pearl's recipe for just about everything was: Turn the oven on to 400 degrees, throw a chicken, potatoes, and vegetables in there, go off and play cards for four hours, and when your kids get home from school, make them wash the blackened pots and pans. Though my grandfather talked about her as if she were Julia Child. For him, nothing was as good as "Mother's." He sat with me late one evening telling me about the symphony that was her macaroni and cheese. I didn't remember it as anything special, so I asked what the big secret was. He said that after putting the packaged macaroni and cheese into a pan, she'd "fan" a layer of American cheese on the top and cook till it just bubbled.

Though my mother was adept at soufflés, her own bread, and fresh-cut pasta, she was famous for almost always forgetting one ingredient. Her cooking sessions were peppered with screams of *"Ahhhh, shit!"* No baking powder in the biscuits, no sugar in the key lime pie. She burned food beyond recognition; her chicken could have easily gone into the witness-protection program. Food was literally lost in her large Garland restaurant-style oven. Many a morning we would come down to see her pulling a blackened rock out of the oven. "I knew I made another potato last Tuesday!" She'd laugh, hurling it across the lawn.

My father would complain. "For-god-sakes-Marsh!" Her absentmindedness worried him. The considerable smoke in the kitchen at every meal made us feel like we were eating in a dream. Plus, he would've liked that potato on Tuesday.

NO DOUBT her mind was often elsewhere. She read like no one I ever knew. With her head in a book, the rest of the world vanished. To get her attention I would drape myself across the chapters.

"Ma, can I go to Barbara's, please?"

She'd mumble a yes, sweeping me off the pages of Doris Lessing, Isaac Bashevis Singer, D. H. Lawrence.

And she'd buy things. We were midway between two

shopping destinations—White Plains and Stamford. And of course there was Manhattan. White Plains was the place I was born, and where her sister lived, so we usually headed there: Bloomingdale's, Saks, Neiman Marcus. She'd make the pilgrimage once a week, to get in touch with her roots and get her roots touched up, buy her groovy clothes, and make sure no one would ever mistake her for a Bedfordian. And I was her copilot for all of the journeys.

I'd turn the radio knob and watch her face. *"How long has this been going on?"* Nothing. *"Still the one that turns my head."* Keep going. *"Summer breeze makes me feel fine . . ."*

My mother would croon along. "In my miiiiind." Bingo.

There was just one thing we had to get around. I was supposed to be in school. I believe it was actually some sort of law.

"Julie was not able to attend school yesterday as she was at Bloomingdale's with me having quiche Lorraine and salad and trying to decide whether a Perry Ellis trench coat made me look more like Jane Fonda in *Klute* or Inspector Clouseau. Please excuse her absence."

In actuality, we concocted illnesses, deaths, doctor's appointments, family emergencies, out-of-town trips. My mother used to say we were like *Naked City.* We had eight million stories.

My grades suffered. The days I actually went to school were miserable, like the dream of going to school undressed, unprepared for the surprise test. Except I was dressed fabulously. And for my mother, that was the important thing. Rather than ask if I was doing okay in school, she would ask if the teacher said I was the prettiest girl in the class, since it was something her mother used to ask her, even when she was in a college lecture hall of three hundred students. I sat in my class looking at a chalkboard of gibberish, pretending I was in a foreign country. I felt sure I'd never catch up and I should just get out of there before it got any worse. Around October, I'd write the year off as a wash. I'd just try again next year, not realizing that starting fresh with none of the skills that everyone else had was not going to work.

"Julie, you look lost," Mrs. Sinapi said in fifth grade.

"I don't get it," I answered truthfully.

"Which part, hon?"

"The, uh, math."

"It's all math."

"Right."

She'd take a minute to go through the same thing she'd just said, more deliberately, stopping every so often for me to give a fake understanding nod, the whole class looking at me or shifting uncomfortably in their seats.

"Now do you have it?"

"Oh, yes," I said convincingly. And then I'd feel ill. I'd pass a note to my best friend, Barbara, and tell her I was leaving. She'd shake her head, pleading no. If I left, she'd have no one to eat lunch with. Math and science and social studies and language arts came easily to Barbara; the lunchroom didn't. I'd let minutes pass and, without looking up, inform the teacher of my combo stomachache/headache. Off to kindly Nurse Donnelly I'd go. She'd ask me if I would like to lie down and then go back to class, or if she should just call Mother Klam. We both knew. Make the call, get it over with.

"Should I have Barbara bring your work home?"

"Ah, no, that's okay."

I was nine and a faker. Was I putting it over on all of these people? In first grade I told my teacher I spoke Hebrew, and when she asked me if I spoke any other languages I said, "Chinese." (They looked alike to me.) She bought it. She went up to my mother at parent-teacher conferences and congratulated her. The next morning I came down to breakfast and everyone was laughing.

"*Shabbat shalom*, Julie. Care to share some of your Hebrew with us?" Brian asked.

"I'd like to hear some Chinese, Hong Kong Fooey," Matt added.

I looked at my mother, who was chuckling. "It's not Julie's fault that woman is an idiot."

"I know Chinese, from Maria!" I said defensively.

Matthew smacked his hand against his forehead. "Maria speaks Spanish!"

"And you don't know that, either!" Brian exclaimed.

I had it in my mind that I was a brilliant actress and that's how I was able to keep the charades going. If only I could have acted smart. I was always behind and lost, and the more behind and lost I got, the more I wanted to stay home or cut out early. I had asthma, so that was the built-in excuse for everything. I was also developing an anxiety disorder and chronic insomnia, so I didn't look so healthy, either.

This added plausibility to my mystery illnesses. If not for the grace of social promotion, I might still be in fourth grade now.

My walrus-looking asthma doctor, who had a deep hatred for the drill-sergeant gym teachers he suffered as a child, reveled in giving me a note at the beginning of every September to excuse me from the whole year's gym classes. Mine was a school where the popular kids were equally good at athletics and academics. I was good at neither, but those who were, as my mother pointed out many times, "dressed like shit."

My mom took great pride in the fact that I came from a long line of hooky players (though she didn't happen to be one of them). But none of them played hooky with their mother. My grandmother used to drive my aunt Phyllis to school and wait till she went into the building before driving off. Meanwhile Phyllis was skipping out the back door. My mother waited for me in front of the school. What a pair. Although I was unable to do long division, I could have had a Ph.D. in accessorizing, and I am fairly certain I was the only fifth-grader at Katonah Elementary School to wear Halston.

Early on, I learned the phrase "popping bonbons," as in "We should be lying on a chaise longue in a pair of fur-trimmed mules, popping bonbons!" At first I thought it was some kind of hunting game, killing little rodents called bonbons. My mother was trying to explain it to me one day when we stumbled upon *Dinner at Eight* on TV. Luscious Jean Harlow held court in her white satin bed with lots of white fluff and feathers, tossing chocolates into her mouth. "THAT'S IT!!!" she yelled. I stared at the screen, committing the image to memory. This is what I should aspire to.

In summer, I would hang out by our pool with my mother and her sisters. Sitting on the diving board, listening to Helen Reddy and Carly Simon, the sun pouring down like honey, I was privy to the continuing education classes taught by the Jewish Gang of Four. There I learned the various methods of wrangling a rich husband and staying "gawjus."

Ranging in age from thirty-one to forty-two, they were all picture perfect, like the publicity stills of Hedy Lamarr and Lana Turner, Ava Gardner and Rita Hayworth. Iris, Phyllis, Marcia, and Mattie. The Smart One, The Pretty One, The Good One, and The Baby, respectively. They tugged at their bikinis, leafed through *Vogue*, sipped iced coffees, puffed True Blues, and chatted, luxuriating in each other's presence and their state of absolute leisure. Occasionally they swam, expertly keeping their hair and makeup from getting messed up in the water.

"Julie, cover your chest," Aunt Iris, the oldest, called over to me. "If you burn there, your skin will be all lizardy by the time you're thirty."

"And your rich husband will dump you for someone younger," added Aunt Phyllis, the second oldest.

"She has lotion on," my mother said in my defense.

"Getting dumped by a rich guy ain't so bad," Aunt Mattie, the youngest, and the smart-ass of the bunch, piped in.

"She'll get a huge settlement and then she can sit in bed all day reading *People* and eating Mallomars."

They continued expounding on the topic for my benefit. Although, they explained carefully, there were face-lifts, eye-lifts, neck-lifts, and boob-lifts, science had yet to discover the cure for that Great Disintegrator of marriages, the sun-damaged chest. Then they'd veer off into their own conversation, forgetting I was there.

"Has anyone seen Annie Dwyer's tits lately?"

"I did. She pulled up her shirt in the middle of Alexander's!"

"She made them too big. She's going to need a lift every six months."

"She's married to a plastic surgeon."

"He's not a plastic surgeon, he's a dermatologist."

"So who's married to the plastic surgeon?"

"Flo Cherney, with the disappearing nose."

"She"—back to Annie Dwyer—"should have saved her money on the tits and gotten rid of the mustache. She looks like Burt Reynolds. I don't care if it's blond."

This was the fascinating world of upside-down "no-logic logic" that my mother and her sisters had perfected with years of practice. I will illustrate this with a quick dramatization of a conversation between my mother and me.

Me: "Wow, Jenny Doe is doing really well. She's a Rhodes scholar, studying theoretical mathematics and counterterrorism, and is very close to discovering the cure for cancer."

My mother: "Yeah, but she has those hairy arms." Right. Exactly. What good is the cure for cancer if you have the arms of a chimp? Conversation over.

Body hair was a big thing with the Smith girls. According to my mother, every woman my father dated before her was bordering on wolf; that they were dogs was understood. They weren't downy; they were furry. And there were many discourses on big butts. During the course of my life I had the good fortune to hear Sandy Cohen's and Gladys Estrin's asses compared to

- Canarsie
- the defensive line of the New York Giants
- a B-52
- some type of object found only in space

In other words, big. As far as the Smith girls were concerned, a big ass, body hair, and poor taste were all punishable crimes.

And though all of the Smith girls experienced the sixties and seventies, buying up the new liberated fashions of the era, the actual liberation somehow passed them by. Even my mother, who fervently supported the ERA at the time, didn't really believe women could run the world. Some women could, just not us. Less attractive women who let their hair go gray and didn't know how to apply blush. More power to them. *Them.*

Summer camp with the kooky sisters would come to a

close and leave me bereft. Not because I'd miss the pool and the tennis court and life lessons from the Smith girls, but because summer was the one time of the year when I was exactly where I was supposed to be. I wasn't getting panic attacks about undone homework and looming report cards, just premature aging and the filling of my future dance card.

My parents were born on opposite sides of the tracks—the IRT's Broadway line, to be exact.

My father, Paul Herbert Klam, was born in 1934 and grew up on Broadway and 150th Street, West Harlem. The Depression was evident in every aspect of his life. His father worked three jobs, his mother worked two, and their small apartment was packed with a revolving slate of relatives who worked no jobs. An only child until he was fifteen, my father took refuge on the fire escape. That was his space; he slept out there when it wasn't raining or snowing, and he rigged a bucket to lower to Kotswinkle's, the store beneath their apartment, where he would get penny candy, comic books, and the occasional egg cream. Dad put his radio up to the window so he could listen to *The Shadow* and *The Lone Ranger*. And though he had friends in the neighborhood, the most significant characters in his memory were the thuggish kids who chased him, the little fat Jewish kid, to and from school. His building was unlocked, so these big kids would follow him into the building and chase him up to the fourth floor, and he'd have to slam his door and lock it before they got there. Once he was inside, they'd bang on the door and yell for him to open up.

He hated them, he hated the city, he hated his parents for never yelling "Hi-yo, Silver!" and getting him the hell out of there.

Ten minutes north and a universe away was Riverdale, an enclave of swanky Jews who had made it out of the shtetl of the Lower East Side. My mother, Marcia Dale Smith, was born in Riverdale in 1938, the third of four daughters—the Fabulous Smith Girls. Her neighborhood was divided into the haves and the have-mores. The Smiths were have-mores. Her mother had bigger diamonds, more furs, and newer Cadillacs than her peers. My mother's childhood, as far as she can recall, was untouched by the Depression. She always thought of herself as rich and pampered and lucky. Though she had two older sisters, she didn't wear hand-me-downs. She took cruises to Europe and wintered in Miami Beach. Her parents had a seemingly endless supply of money. And though she was comfortable, she doesn't remember feeling happy. "We didn't think about that one way or the other," she recalls. "That's something new."

Her material comforts didn't come without a price. She had a job to do, and it was to marry—someone. She had been dating a guy in college who was funny and handsome.

"So what was his deal?" I asked her later.

"He was poor!" she said. He was going to college on the GI Bill and working as a cigarette "detail man"—someone who delivers and sets up the products at stores. When he met with a career counselor at NYU, they told him to stick with the cigarette job. "He just wasn't that . . . *equipped*," my mother said. "But because he had a heartbeat," she said, "my mother wanted me to marry him. She said she would subsidize him."

My mother said she didn't love him. Her mother didn't react. "What, do you just want me to be married?" she asked her mother, outraged.

"Yes, I do!" her mother said.

My mom was very aware that her having a date on Saturday night was critical to her success in the family. If she didn't have plans and her parents had friends over for a card game, she did not show her face.

"It wasn't like a posted rule," she remembered. "My parents never said, 'Don't come out of your room!' But we knew we weren't welcome to say hello. Or make noise." Pretend you're out on a date.

On her luckier Saturdays, she might be out with the guy with the blue Cadillac. He was handsome but "dumb as a box of rocks." She thought she could get past his lack of braininess until he told her he was making her a painting—"and he was just finishing the sevens." It was paint-by-numbers, pre-kitsch.

The summer after my mother graduated from NYU, her parents let her know that time was ticking, like when the Wicked Witch of the West turned the hourglass upside down with Dorothy locked in the tower. If she fell in love, great; if not, Artie Oberman's son, the morbidly obese shoestore owner, was available. She needed to find true love fast, or she'd be stuck with a flying monkey and a lifetime of free shoes in up to size 15EEE.

Trying to increase my mother's pool of eligible men, her

parents urged her to join the swingin', happenin' El Dorado Beach Club in New Rochelle, New York, conveniently located next door to the stately Greentree Country Club, where her parents were members. She dated three men there, but very quickly zeroed in on Mr. Wonderful. My father was handsome, funny, and much taller than she had thought when she first met him. ("He was sitting down, and all of his height is in his legs.") So though he had little money, he was smart and ambitious, with good prospects. A fine catch. The courtship was brief; my mother knew she loved him the night he said he was taking her to the Broadway show *Kiss Me, Kate* but instead took her to his parents' living room, where they stared at the propped-up album cover and listened to the soundtrack. A few months later, on January 31, 1960, they got hitched.

My father had been married very briefly before, to a British girl whose father was a vice president at Shell Oil. "He was the only Jew!" my father said.

Her mother was Church of England. "She was kind of chilly," my father recalled, "and was always clanking a big tumbler of whiskey."

When he met the Smiths, he was very moved by the warmth and closeness of the family. "I wanted to be a part of it."

His first wedding had been a huge affair at the Essex House on Central Park South, so he wanted to keep this one small. The ceremony and reception were held in my grandmother's house. Mom wore a tea-length dress instead of the ivory duchess satin ball gown with the twelve-foot train that her older sisters had worn, but she didn't care. Nor did she care that they had to pry my father away from the Giants playoff game on the upstairs TV to say his vows. They were two cake-toppin' lovebirds, completely smitten with each other as they headed off to the Bahamas for their honeymoon. When they returned, real life began, sort of. They were immediately moved into an apartment my mother's parents had found and furnished for them. The refrigerator was stocked and their family had now grown to include a maid, who went by the single name of Fabiola.

As was the standard of the time, my mother had gone from living with her parents to living with her husband, never alone. She worked for a bit at IBM as a newlywed, and happily quit when her first baby was arriving. Her brush with employment was just that. She had gone to NYU business school because that's where the men were. Even though she tested into the insanely competitive Hunter High School, she was sent to Yonkers High because Hunter was all-girls. She wasn't angered by it, she just followed the plan. No surprise, her IBM career was less than soul-satisfying and not heartbreaking to leave behind.

To accommodate their growing family, they decided to move to a house in White Plains, where she had Brian and, two years later, another son, Matthew. My mother had everything she wanted. Her mother and sisters were minutes away, she adored her husband and sons and Fabiola. After another two years she got pregnant for the third time. Now things were about to get really good.

A little before noon on Tuesday, October 25, 1966, my mother's water broke. She decided to call her mother, who was minutes away, rather than my father, who was at a meeting in downtown Manhattan, to take her to the hospital. She packed a bag and waited. Fifteen minutes, a half-hour, forty-five minutes passed. The phone rang. It was her mother.

"Can Aunt Nina borrow your white mink stole?"

"Ma, you're supposed to take me to the hospital!"

"Oh, Jesus!" my grandmother replied. "I'll be out front in ten minutes. Bring the stole for Nina, willya?"

She eventually arrived, and so did I. My older brothers, Brian and Matthew, had the same fair-haired looks as my father's side of the family, the Klams. The third time around my mother expected more of the same. My name was going to be Jason or something; they didn't even have a girl's name picked out because the possibility was so unlikely. And then (cue the harp glissando) she had a *girl*. And not just a girl (cue the Hallelujah Chorus), she had a SMITH GIRL. I had her brown hair (we'd fix that later), her strong features, her long build (and eventually, her bunions). My mother was elated; she finally had someone on her team. I was named Julie. (It was the year of *Dr. Zhivago* and Julie Christie; if I'd been a boy, they might've called me Omar.)

My mother was quite comfortable in White Plains, near her sisters and her parents, and her Bloomingdale's, but my father wanted to keep his horses at home. He always had this fantasy that his parents had kidnapped him from Montana ranchers or Sioux Indians. He longed to go live in his imaginary ancestral land, but Upper Westchester would just have to do.

The new house was a sprawling, nine-bedroom affair built in 1790 by the Lyons family, wealthy landowners. Over time, the land connected to the house shrank from half of Bedford, New York, to eight acres. Though it sure didn't feel like it to me at the time, we hadn't really moved that far, geographically. But demographically, we had jumped planets. We had gone from a street where all the kids played outside at night and ran into the back doors of one another's houses to this bucolic WASP enclave where you couldn't even see any other kids or neighbors or other houses. We were physically isolated, and being one of only three Jewish families in the town—not counting the (Ralph) Laurens—socially alienated. Now it was us kids' turn to feel kidnapped.

There are images from childhood that, seen from an adult perspective, are not nearly so awesome. In my memory, the stairs of my elementary school were like those steps Rocky triumphed over, but when I saw them later, there were only about six or seven of them. The Katonah house, however, was overwhelming from any viewpoint, any height, any age. It seemed so big because it *was* so big. The grounds included a recently resurfaced tennis court amid stately two-hundred-year-old pines, a Gatsby-era swimming pool surrounded by whispering poplar trees, a stable and corral, and horses to prance and gambol all around them. Several lush English gardens dotted the landscape, as well as a cozy picturesque stone groundskeeper's cottage (which my parents would later rent out to the seventies version of a groundskeeper—a tennis pro). The house had four floors and more than twenty-five rooms. It had the same details as Van Cortlandt Manor, Philipsburg Manor, and any number of historic homes I later visited on school field trips: the wide-board floors, the wavy glass windows, the irregular ceiling heights, and secret passageways. It even had the added accents of electric buzzers installed in each room in the 1920s as a "modern" way to call one's servants, and a dirt-floor basement room with a creaky door into which somebody had carved the words KEEP OUT under a scary skull-like face. My parents left the warning and turned it into their wine cellar.

There's no sense trying to deny it: the house was grand. But for a family of five, including two older brothers of nine and seven and a four-year-old girl who loved her old house the way it was, jammed between two other houses each with a four-year-old girl, it was just too big, like the setting for *The Shining*. I felt like I needed a miner's light and a canteen to traverse the passageways. There was a lot of "Follow the sound of my voice" to get us kids from one room in the house to my mother.

My parents were do-it-yourselfers. Rather than call in hordes of repair people and designers, they took on the tasks themselves . . . in theory. In actuality, things just didn't get done. They were in a perpetual state of exhaustion. There was so much to manage: the house, the grounds, the kids, the animals (two horses, four dogs, three cats, twenty-five chickens, two roosters). And that wasn't all. As country dwellers, we became accustomed to seeing a wide array of wildlife on our property: deer, squirrels, chipmunks. Our grounds were an ornithologist's dream, with pileated woodpeckers, evening grosbeaks, and red-tailed hawks, and an entomologist's dream, too: there were loads of bugs. My own personal nightmare was the snakes. When I say we became accustomed to the wildlife, I don't mean that I did. The whole *Wild Kingdom* experience never sat very well with me, especially the way the animals tended to overstep their boundaries, particularly those of the walls of our house. We had eight entrances into our home and countless gaps that critters could slip in through. Once a snake found its way into our formal dining room, and from then on, for many years, I was never without boots in the house. In the morning my feet went directly from my bed into a pair of Wellies. I'd wear them in the bathroom, down the stairs, and out the front door, just to avoid the now very real possibility that my naked foot might encounter a snake.

My brother Matt still gets green when he recalls the morning he put a coat on to go feed the horses and put his hand in the pocket to find a living, breathing, wriggling mouse, which ran straight up his sleeve. Matt seemed to suffer an inordinate number of similar brushes with creepiness. Like the morning he found a waterlogged rat the size of a large dachshund in one of the horse's water buckets (it had eaten a lot of poison and was very, very thirsty). Brian discovered a tarantula-like spider that had laid eggs in his desert boot. I myself sat on a wasp's nest, and we were all severely allergic to the poison ivy that dominated our play areas. Despite all this, the worst incident, we on the Committee of Childhood Terror agree, was the bat.

In a house as large as ours, many things were bound to go wrong at once. My mother would go to change a lightbulb in the den and on the way there get caught up in ten million other things—a picture that needed hanging, a paint can left open, an unemptied dustpan—and suddenly it would be midnight when she'd crawl off to bed, the den still dark. My parents were both so harried with the upkeep of the house that I kept uncharacteristically quiet about my unending checklist of fears most of the time. But when a bat flew into my bedroom, my screams were so loud that they echoed through the house and the woods, and I'm fairly certain my aunt heard me back in White Plains.

My entire family burst in to assess the situation in their uniquely useless way. My father shouted something deeply threatening to a bat, like "Cocksucker-motherfucker . . ." My brothers both grabbed tennis racquets, attempting to forehand, backhand, and serve the intruder. My mother fell into an uncontrollable hysterical laughing fit. It seemed to go on for an eternity, like the spinning-out of a car in an accident. Finally the bat flew into the screen in my window and my father slammed down the window, caging it. Its claws stuck into the screen, splayed out like a science-lab project waiting for dissection. Except it was alive—and stayed that way for a long, long time. The worst part was that it remained in that window, on that screen, slowly, agonizingly dying for weeks. I trained myself to never look in that area of the window. When it finally perished and dropped off, my father, wearing oven mitts, removed it, wrapped it in newspaper, and threw it in the trash. Some funeral.

Aside from just the ghost of the dead bat, I was fairly convinced the house was haunted. My mother, who had liberated herself from a full-time maid when we moved, was so incredibly messy that when the ghosts moved or removed something, no one else would notice, but I was keeping a close watch. After we'd been living there for about five years, a lovely elderly couple walked up our driveway. Their car, it seemed, had broken down, and they needed a phone. As if in a bad 1930s horror movie, the old man, it turned out, had grown up in our very house. He walked through the rooms like a medium in a séance, announcing, "Sister played her harp here." And, "There used to be a Japanese maple out this window." (There still was.)

As he walked up the stairs, he went on to describe the posh affairs that took place in the house in the 1920s, named all the swells who'd attended, and then he turned the corner and walked into my brother Brian's room. He looked around at the Walter Payton and Björn Borg posters, closed his eyes for a moment, and intoned, "Mother died in here." Matt and I loved that. We'd walk in at night before Brian went to bed, join hands, eyes wide, Norma Desmond–like, and repeat the old-timer's eerie declaration. Brian would throw some balled-up sweatsocks at us. It never got old.

There we were in the castle with the moat and the ghosts and the moors and the snakes. Our relatives who thought ponies brought us our mail addressed things to:

Klam Family
Katonah, NY

And we would get the mail. Katonah was not White Plains, and it sure as hell wasn't Riverdale. Those places were suburban, this was disturbingly rural: The Boonies.

It was no wonder, then, that my mother sought refuge in my company, even at the risk of derailing my fledgling academic career. I'm sure on some level she wondered what exactly her education had gotten her. I know she felt some secret delight in saving me from the school I was hating; her mother would never have done that. For my part, well, she was my mother, but she was also the most fun person to play with—hilarious, rich, and every bit the glamorous princess. And she always picked up the check at lunch.

There was that nagging issue that I'd be entering the world of the 1980s, not the 1950s, and by now my deficiencies were glaringly apparent. I was as ready for the future as one of those bugs that live for only one day. There was going to be some kind of payback for all those outings, even beyond the fact that I was the first person in my family to graduate in the bottom ten percent of my class.

Three

Hey, You Guys, Wait Up!

My crummy grades and painfully average SAT scores got me into exactly two out of the twenty-six schools I applied to. They were the University of Maryland, where Brian had just graduated from, and Bard College, where, my brothers told me, no one shaved their legs.

"Do you want that?" my mother asked with a "something smells bad" face. Her preferred image of college was coed parties and boys and FUN, not protests and feminist poetry. For my part, I didn't know what the hell I wanted (hence the twenty-six applications).

Driven by my fear of the unknown and a strong attachment to my blue-star-handled Lady Gillette, I chose Maryland. I figured Brian, who had once held my hand when we crossed streets, would be a great nearby emergency number. I didn't apply to the University of New Hampshire, Matthew's school, because he didn't want me there. "You'd be pointing at me on the quad," Matthew said, "and I'd have to pretend I didn't see it."

MY MARYLAND EXPERIENCE boiled down to one year of me working hard for the first time in my life, making the dean's list, and being able to transfer closer to my mommy.

Maryland was a fine place for someone. It was well known for its parties, which I didn't go to. Less well known was that the Swenson's on campus delivered something they called the Survival Kit. It was the only tip the RA gave that I actually found useful. This fine concoction came in a sizable refrigerator bag. For four dollars and fifty cents, plus tip, you got a luscious pint of ice cream (the flavor of your choice, say, Swiss chocolate), a to-go coffee cup brimming with thick hot fudge, another to-go cup of freshly pressed sprinkles or chopped nuts, and an entire can of Reddi-wip. I didn't drink, so this was my version of letting loose. How they didn't mention this in the University of Maryland viewbook was a mystery to me.

The summer after my freshman year, my Survival Kit, Hadassah-lady brisket arms and I mailed a transfer application to NYU. I waited and waited and waited. By the end of July, I needed to make a decision about Maryland, so I called NYU.

"Let's see," the woman on the phone said, making paper-shifting noises. "Here it is. Mmm. Mmm. Mmm-hmm. Okay, you didn't get in."

"What?" Me, incredulous. "Why?"

"Uh, your grades aren't high enough?" the admissions person asked, rather than told, me. I felt a window open.

"I got a 3.8 and a 3.9."

"You did?"

"Don't you have my transcript?"

"Let's see"—more shuffling noises—"here it is! Yes! Wow, okay. Okay. Uh-huh . . . yeah, you can come here."

I had always imagined college admissions as a big oak-paneled room filled with tweed-clad professors spending hours reviewing a single applicant before one of them banged the gavel and declared, "*I deem thee ACCEPTED.*"

"So, which school do you want? Do you know what we have?" she asked, like I was choosing the color of a field coat from the L.L. Bean catalogue. Yes, I'd like, first choice, Saddle Brown, but if they are out of stock I'll take Mallard Green.

"Tisch School of the Arts," I said.

"What major?" she asked. "Film or acting or something?"

"Film, please." And we'll take the check, too, when you have the chance.

NYU Film School was everything I dreamed it would be. Here was a place where my obsession with film and pop culture was looked on not as a quirky aberration but a legitimate field of study. Reading through the catalogue of course descriptions that centered around watching movies like *Flashdance* and *For a Few Dollars More* gave me such a euphoric, pounding glee. It was like I'd put something over on the world of education, and I was careful not to say too much.

As giddy as I was, though, there was a significant disconnect between what I had been raised to do, which was nothing, and what I was doing, attending a highly competitive university. Part of me was going to NYU because it was closer to my mother, but another part hoped that I would become some type of professional person. I was lost again.

The NYU joke was that the school color was black (clothes, hair, nails, eyeliner). The average student read Kafka, drank coffee, listened to alternative music, and went to therapy. I happily wore loads of black, read Kafka (especially when someone was watching), and listened to alternative music that seemed to involve a lot of Ians (Curtis, MacKaye, and McCullough, from Joy Division, Minor Threat, and Echo & the Bunnymen, respectively). So why not therapy?

My therapist, Margot Fredericks, was not what I expected. Being a big fan of the movie *Ordinary People*, I looked forward to a female Judd Hirsch.

What I got was a striking young woman who resembled a high school field hockey captain, with ruddy cheeks and natural blond streaks running through her long hair. Her office on Central Park West (or Cuckoo's Nest Mile) overlooked the park. She seemed only a couple of years older than me, but worlds away.

When the session started, Margot sat across from me, saying nothing, and I burst into tears and cried for what seemed like hours. Before the session I had been worried that she wouldn't think there was anything wrong with me. No problem there.

I paid close attention to everything about her because she seemed like someone I'd be wise to emulate. I found that going to therapy depressed me, but Margot was so sharp I couldn't resist getting her take on everything. I remember taking the C train home after a session, thinking, "I'm in therapy with the smartest person in the world." I figured I'd stick with it, at least for a little while. Until I was out of the woods.

There were so many adjustments, so much to settle in to. It was difficult to get NYU housing as a transfer student, so I looked around the East Village for an affordable place to live. The thought of my living in Alphabet City made my father quite ill, so he decided that he'd buy an apartment in a "nice" neighborhood as an investment, which I would live in during school and then move out of when I graduated. He would pay the maintenance and utilities, and I would work for my spending money.

After settling on a charming parlor studio in a brownstone on West Eightieth, at Columbus, an apartment that could have fit easily in my bedroom in Katonah, I went about looking for a job. I worked first at Häagen-Dazs, until I got so fat my mother said she'd pay me not to work there, and then moved on to Banana Republic. This was back when Banana Republic carried safari clothes, not urban chic. The one I worked at had a big jeep and a fake molded plastic baobab tree in the middle of the store and blasted 1930s jungle-movie music.

My primary responsibility was folding shirts on boards and placing them in stacks so neat they would've pleased Joan Crawford. Not two minutes after I'd finished carefully stacking, some Upper West Side stroller mom would waltz over and start tearing through the pile for a medium, only to decide that she didn't want it, not in medium or small or large or extra-large. She couldn't decide this from the top shirt; she had to wreck my work. I stood it as long I could, just under four months.

I worked there with my best friend at the time, a guy named Thom, gay, hilarious, no threat. I was really terrified about dating. I felt that being involved with a man meant being swallowed up by his needs, the way I (probably incorrectly) perceived my parents. And anyway, no one was beating down my door. I got asked out by one guy in my Semiotics of Cinema class (taught by a serious nose-picker). I told the guy I'd go out with him and then I said I had a boyfriend. All in one breath. That was nice of me. I sure wasn't my mother flirting with the guy in the bank. I had a crush on one guy, though. He was Jewish (very novel for me) and funny, and he lived at home with his mother in the legendary Apthorp building. His father, a blockbuster movie producer, lived in Los Angeles. One day, after I helped him on his final film project, I screwed up the courage to ask him out, but he said he was already seeing someone. I would never do that again.

Before my junior year I took another detour off the map I'd been drawn—the one with Start and a line to end with a rich husband. At a lunch with my mother and Mattie at the American Festival Café at Rockefeller Center, I made a startling announcement. First I waited for Mattie to finish picking the little bits of bacon out of her salad.

"I applied for an internship on the Letterman show."

"You're never going to get that," Mattie said. "Everyone wants that."

My mother sat quietly, not wanting to dismiss me outright but completely agreeing with Mattie.

"Why shouldn't I get it? I'm an NYU film school student," I argued.

They both frowned at me. Mattie shook her head.

"You think I'm a dope?" I asked rhetorically.

"Do whatever you want. It doesn't cost anything, does it?" my mother said. "To apply, I mean."

A month after sending in my forms, my phone remained quiet, but then a letter arrived, in an NBC envelope.

Dear Julie,

I've been trying to call you to come in for an interview for an internship position but I keep getting a wrong number (a Hispanic woman who's never heard of you). Please call me if you're still interested.

Best,

Susie Marriott

Internship Coordinator

Late Night with David Letterman

I looked at the copy of my application that was enclosed. I had written my telephone number incorrectly, one number off. I was very good at sabotaging my efforts to move up in the world by messing up some detail. My subconscious, it seemed, was on the Smith girls' team.

Instead of paging Dr. Freud, I called Susie and set up an interview, apologizing furiously for the oversight. She thought it was hilarious; it was a comedy show, after all.

I went to the interview, and the waiting area was packed with prospective interns, including a set of twins who said hello to Steve O'Donnell, the head writer, when he breezed through the office. I'd recognized him from his appearances on the show and from a *New York* magazine article about the *Late Night* writers. As I looked around, my mother's voice in my head said, "No way. No how."

The producer must not have heard it, because I got hired, initially as a talent intern and then, at Dave's request, as his personal intern. Mattie said that after that she never saw me the same way again. Maybe I wasn't one of the Smith girls after all.

Every day was a high point. I assisted Dave's personal assistant with the running of his life. Along with buying his clothes and getting his lunch, I got to watch Dave come into and out of his office, making observations about things ranging from Don Zimmer's expression while being interviewed, to soft towels versus abrasive towels, to the ghastliness of a certain actress. He would just walk around saying the kinds of things millions of people heard him say on TV every night. He was brilliant, kind, generous, down-to-earth, and hilarious. He pretty much ruined me for any future work. In addition to Dave, I got very close to Steve O'Donnell and one of the staff writers, Adam Resnick, who became like a brother to me. Steve, Adam, and I all lived on the Upper West Side and often walked home from the office at 30 Rockefeller Center together, with Steve commenting on the sights of the city and stopping in smelly dollar stores to purchase potentially comic objects for bits on the show.

One balmy night we were walking up Columbus Avenue and one of the restaurants had its glass doors opened to the street. I looked at the man seated closest to us. It was Bill Murray. I smiled at him. He smiled back, and then he recognized Steve and jumped out the window and started walking with us. It's not easy going back to civilian life after that.

I had been on the show a couple of times (one episode was the fabled Sonny and Cher reunion show) and gone to dinner with Dave (once) and chatted with Jerry Seinfeld and Teri Garr at the Christmas party, but it wasn't that. I felt like a competent person and I was in the biggest of ponds, surrounded by whale sharks.

At the end of the semester, I reluctantly went back and finished school, receiving a bachelor of fine arts. The speaker at our Tisch School graduation ceremony? Anthony "Zorba the Greek" Quinn, whose name was not quite synonymous with academia, but somehow seemed appropriate to the school.

With my degree and the successful Letterman internship under my belt, I was ready to set the world on fire. Not so much on fire, really, as set it at room temperature. I was still not clear about what the point of my working was. I knew the idea was for me to be self-reliant, but I didn't understand why I would want to be. It sounded awfully lonely. Margot and I talked about it.

"There is a satisfaction you get from taking care of yourself," she said.

"But isn't there also a satisfaction in getting someone to take care of you?" I countered.

"Think about it," she said, uncrossing her legs, the universal therapy signal for "Time up."

I had been getting six hundred dollars a month as an allowance from my dad. It was due to phase out when I secured a job. Mattie, who'd been a social worker for the Department of Welfare in the South Bronx, used to compare me to her clients. She said they were getting welfare for doing nothing and getting a job would only be to their detriment. They would lose all the benefits, and few of them were equipped to get the kind of job that would even come close to equaling their welfare checks. Bingo. It just didn't pay. My brothers, it should be noted, had no such arrangement. No allowance. No home purchased for their use.

A former professor of mine who didn't know about my fear of the workforce recommended me for a job; I was none too secure on my first interview. The position was assistant to the editor in chief of *Interview* magazine.

The pretty, petite, soft-spoken editor with a warm smile was doing her best to find something worthwhile in my poorly padded résumé.

June 30, 1983–August 30, 1983 Loehmann's Mt. Kisco, New York. Sales Associate.

Duties included displaying merchandise, assisting customers, assisting the manager, having lunch with my mother, hiding Ralph Lauren blazers for my mother to buy me when she came in to get me for lunch, comparing my ass in the mirror of the dressing room to other asses.

She gently began to interview me.

"So, you went to NYU?" She smiled. This of course was my cue to talk about something: Why NYU? What did I like about it, or not? What prepared me, et cetera?

Instead I said, "Mmm-hmm."

"And you have a film degree? That sounds fun!"

"I watched a lot of movies." It was a complete sentence, you had to give me that.

"Why are you interested in getting into magazines?"

She had me there. I couldn't say what was true, which was, "I'm not. Who's interested in magazines? I want to work in movies but I went out to Los Angeles and I was scared because it was too far away from my mommy. I'm only here because a film professor who I liked knew about the job."

"I like reading magazines."

"Do you read *Interview*?"

"No." I didn't want to lie. Truth is, I found it a very cumbersome magazine to hold, something I planned to correct when I worked there.

She was looking for the IDIOT stamp on my forehead when she made one final attempt to find some sign of why her colleague had recommended me.

"Do you have any questions?"

Questions? What? Actually, yeah, I did have a question. It was getting dangerously close to my dinnertime and these people were still hard at work, running around the office with no sign of sliding down the dinosaur's tail in sight. What was that about?

"What are the hours?" I asked innocently.

There are very few interviewers who spark up when you inquire about quittin' time.

"We start at nine-thirty and stay until we get the job done."

I flinched. Get the job done? When is that? That could be really late. Then I'd be hungry, and I didn't like to ride the subway too late, so cab fare would have to be deducted. It wasn't looking like the right opportunity for me.

A week later I was still trying to figure out how I was going to break it to her that I wouldn't take the job when I found out, to my real surprise, that I didn't get it. Phew! Next? I saw a movie shortly after that in which the character was interviewing and she said, "I'm not afraid of hard work, Mr. Baxter." I remember thinking I would use that line. I wasn't *afraid* of hard work; I just didn't want to do it. It wasn't like I had committed a crime.

A few months later I had another job interview. This one went better, because the guy I interviewed with was on the phone the whole time and couldn't hear the cluelessness in my answers. Fred Goldberg was a very handsome, very gay talent agent whose hair was blown out to Barry Manilow perfection. I would assist him at his swanky office at Fifty-seventh and Seventh, which was a ten-minute subway ride from my house, an ideal commute. It seemed like it was going to be a cream-puff job. Talk to celebs and get paid. It was the eighties and his office represented all the A-listers: William Hurt, Kevin Kline, Bruce Willis, Morgan Freeman, Melanie Griffith, Raul Julia, Christopher Reeve. My job was to set up auditions for Fred's clients, send them scripts, and get submissions and headshots to casting agents. Every Monday there was a lunch meeting with free food, including beverages and enormous cookies. Friday-morning meetings included doughnuts and muffins. I loved it. I'd never had cranberry and orange together in one muffin. It was like living in the pages of *People* magazine, complete with catering. Except when it wasn't. Like when the phone would ring.

"Fred Goldberg's office."

"Hi, it's Harvey Keitel."

"Hi, Harvey, let me see if he's in." Press hold. Fred would stick his puss out of his office.

"It's Harvey Keitel?"

"Are you asking me?"

"No, it's him. Would you like to speak to him?"

"Yes. YES!" He'd shake his head at my complete ineptitude, muttering under his breath.

Pick up the phone. "Hi, Harvey, one moment please."

Press transfer, then hold, then 646. The phone would ring in Fred's office.

Fred would pick up the call. "Hi, Harv . . . Hello? Hello?

"There is nobody there." His voice would be layered in a thick coating of *I hate you*, and he would glare at me. I would stare at the phone in disbelief.

"CALL HIM BACK!" he'd yell. I'd riffle through the Rolodex, the work of one of the fifty-odd previous assistants, and of course there would be no Harvey Keitel card.

"Do you know his phone number?" I would ask, my eyes drying with anxiety.

"Oh my GOD!" he would say to no one. "Do you want me to dial it myself, too?"

He would slam his door and I'd sit frozen for a few minutes before returning to my work.

I wasn't prepared for this. I probably wasn't prepared for anything.

All of my correspondence was done on the latest technological advance in communication—the electric typewriter. If you typed a letter and made a mistake, you had to yank the sheet out and start all over again. There was a correcting ribbon, but Fred didn't like how corrections looked. The more I got yelled at, the more mistakes I made, until a letter looked something like this:

Deakt HJshko,

I am podhgfbse dost submit the foLSOEihn iwbAfo ftor the ROLE of Annda,

HEATHER G#FTM

Sneiceryl,

He yelled and threw things. Not at me, unless I was in the path of the object he was hurling. He blew thick puffs of smoke in my asthmatic face. When I mistakenly sent flowers to an actor at the wrong theater in London (apparently there is more than one Shakespeare theater there) he stomped over to my desk, seething, still wearing his sunglasses even though he'd been inside for several hours.

"Can't you do *anything* right?"

"Wha—?"

"Do I have to do *everything*?"

"I don't think—"

"I *know* you don't!" He called the office manager into his office and slammed the door. I waited at my desk for half an hour, until finally I couldn't take it anymore. I got up and knocked and opened the door. They both stared at me in disbelief.

"Are you firing me? Because if you're not, I'm quitting," I said, mustering my first ounce of courage since I'd been there.

"I haven't decided yet," he said, filing a nail. "I'm thinking of firing you."

I collected my purse and sweater and shopping bag with sneakers and went through the glass doors to the waiting area, where an actress sat, Fred's next appointment. She was about to be dumped by him, too. It was December 23. Merry Christmas and God bless us every one!

Snow had begun to fall and I felt elated. I was free. I dialed my mother from a pay phone and yelled, "Great news! I got fired!"

My mother was weirdly uncelebratory.

"Did you get another job?"

"Ma, he fired me five minutes ago. I didn't get another job yet." I was stunned. "You can't get a job like a Coach bag! Here, I'll take this one!" What she didn't know about working was almost as bad as what I didn't know. Except that she didn't have to do it.

It made me so mad. I felt like she should have run to my aid, and clearly she was expecting me to get back on the horse. I had tried to work, but I couldn't do it. Shouldn't I be supported in my decision to retire?

My mother had one job when she got out of college, and then she got pregnant with my brother. But seeing as I wasn't married, I wasn't eligible for that plan.

It was as if they thought I had a choice. I am here to tell you, I did not. Not only wasn't anyone proposing to me, no one was asking me to dinner. But it wasn't just me; none of my friends had boyfriends. I was twenty-two, the age my mother had been when she got married, and I was still excited when *It's the Great Pumpkin, Charlie Brown* came on TV. I had no interest in being an adult in the real world. Those were the people who yelled at me.

When I went off to college, my mother started taking some classes herself. She'd been to an astrologer who told her she'd make a good psychic healer. The practice, as she told me, "involves how the chakras take in Universal Energy, which goes up the body, feeding organs and emotions. When you experience trauma, you block the energy from coming in. That protects you from the bad feeling, but it also blocks the good feeling. If you can let that energy run clearly, you will have more of your life's experiences in a true way and thus be your True Self, rather than the self you've created to protect you from the world."

Something about the idea clicked with her. The group of nine women she took the classes with became one of the first group of graduates from the Barbara Brennan School of Healing. Now the school has a thousand students, as well as locations in Europe and Asia. After graduating, she taught and supervised and became dean of the senior class. It was a very exciting time for her, and she really came into her own. She still went to Bergdorf's, but now she bought flowy skirts and sparkly scarves instead of cruisewear.

Being fired propelled me to consider joining her in her work. For a brief time I thought, "Hey, these goofballs are really nice and sincere and no one throws scripts at anyone's heads. Maybe this is for me." One weekend I went and visited her at the school in the Hamptons. She was a powerhouse. When we came out of the elevator, swarms of students came up to her, hugging her and holding her hands like the aliens around Richard Dreyfuss in *Close Encounters of the Third Kind*. I stepped back and thought, "How . . . ?" She was making money, and she was loving it. While at the weekend, I met a guy, a student at the school, named Lamar. Formerly a lawyer, he'd gone to Princeton, and he was cute (at least compared with the other male student, who wore a feathered headdress). He was definitely a Healer Boy. His dialogue was littered with so much New Age jargon that I had trouble having a conversation with him. But when he asked me for my number, I gave it to him.

The following weekend he came into Manhattan to see his father and asked me for a date. Except he didn't call it a date, he called it a "journey of the white goddess within" or something like that. Upon entering my apartment, he was immediately seized with a writhing pain I can describe only as a kind of Captain-James-T.-Kirk-throbbing-temple-can't-speak-can't-stand-it type of pain. The little bit I knew about Lamar made me suspect that what he was suffering from was not something for the 911 people to handle, but perhaps the witch doctor from Bugs Bunny. Sure enough, he threw himself over to my couch and, contorting his face, mimed pulling something out of his stomach, like a magician with endless colored scarves, jerking and yanking and wrenching, and in a final dramatic flourish he dropped his psychic gizzards on my floor and doubled over.

"Is that going to stain?" I yelled, pointing at my carpet. He quickly picked it up and made a hasty exit.

I called my mother and told her what happened.

"Jesus, some of these people . . ." she said.

He left a message on my machine later, apologizing for his severe psychic intestinal distress, what I would later refer to as the sausage-link trick.

SO MUCH FOR FINDING MYSELF with the happy voodoo people. I was longing for the concrete world of entertainment people. After a good go at procrastinating, I made some calls to some of my agency contacts. I told them I needed a job, but no more ego people, no more being intimidated and threatened. A couple of days later I got my first interview. It wasn't exactly what I had asked for, but at least I could someday tell my grandkids I had been interviewed by Barbra Joan Streisand.

She was getting ready to do *Prince of Tides* and needed a second (or third or fourth) assistant. By this point I knew a little more about interviews and being prepared. I'd seen enough desperate actors go in and out of Fred's office, and the ones who made it were always strong, confident, and wearing killer outfits.

I walked the ten blocks from my apartment to Barbra's wearing head-to-toe Donna Karan and feeling totally uncomfortable. Getting fired had sent me into an eating frenzy, and I was so bloated that the skirt pinched a red mark into my gut. The stockings, which my mother had purchased at Syms, were irregular—one leg was very small and tight, and the other was loose like sweatpants. I was wearing a white cashmere blazer that was dirty before they finished putting the label on it. Walking there, I was in a cold sweat, and by the time I arrived I was in the midst of a full-blown panic attack.

Fortunately, Barbra Streisand's building was right next to my therapist Margot's. If I needed to I could run over after the interview for an emergency session.

I went in and was directed to the top floor. The elevator opened into a small hallway with only one door. I wiped off my sweaty hand before ringing the bell, and I was brought into the outer sanctum. Moments later Barbra swept in and introduced herself. "Hello, I'm Barbra Streisand." *Oh my God*, I thought, *what a thing to say.*

We sat across from each other on her creamy couch. She was wearing a gray cashmere sweatsuit and no makeup. She was like one of my aunts mixed with Louis B. Mayer. She looked like someone's Jewish mother, but she was one of the most powerful women in the entertainment industry. My ass-kissing sensors were all screwed up. Celeb or mom? She asked me about NYU—her son was there when I was. "Do you know Jason Gould?" she said, pronouncing his name very clearly and loudly. All Jewish mothers are the same. Do you know my son? Don't you think he's the greatest thing since sliced challah?

Of course I knew Barbra Streisand and Elliott Gould's son's name, and Bob Dylan's son's name, and Francis Ford Coppola's son's name, and Martin Scorsese's daughter's name. Only Cathy Scorsese knew *my* name, though. She and I were friends. In addition to the legacies, Adam Sandler was in my college class, and he was already making a name for himself at *Saturday Night Live*.

"I know of him." Stupid answer.

"He's friends with Jesse Dylan, Bob Dylan's son," she prompted, another opportunity for me to say, "Oh yeah, he's the best!" I knew someone who was friends with Jesse Dylan, that was all I could give her.

"I sort of know *him*. I know Joe Stevens, who knows Jesse. They went to Beverly High together."

Why hadn't I socialized more? I took a lot of pride in the

fact that I didn't sniff up to the famous people's kids. Cathy Scorsese and I had been in several classes together, and she made friends with me first.

My mind was drifting; I was doing okay, not great, not terrible, and then it hit me. People Who Need People Love Soft as an Easy Chair The Way We Were. One minute I was being interviewed for a job, the next I was sitting next to Elvis Presley. I was one big puddle of flop sweat, lost my mind and couldn't locate it. At the preinterview with her producing partner I had boasted "an embarrassingly retentive memory." And here I could barely give her my name. What skills did I have? Clearly being at ease with legends was not one of them.

She looked down at my résumé and asked about my David Letterman internship. "He's cute." She smiled. "What's his story?" What did she mean? Was she asking if Dave was available to date?

David Letterman was the best boss I ever had. He was a great guy, really funny and caring. He felt like one of my brothers, not scary. Barbra asked for his number so she could call him for a reference.

I called my mother from a pay phone and said, "Barbra Streisand is going to call David Letterman to talk about me."

"Oy," she said.

I walked home and found my answering machine filled with messages from the yentas, asking how Ms. Streisand looked. How was her skin? Her hair? What did she wear? How did she smell? Thin or fat?

I couldn't talk. I didn't want to go back there. I prayed to

God that I wouldn't get the job, but also that I wouldn't not get the job. And God answered my prayer because I never heard from them. Not a yes or a no. You could say that not hearing is a no, but it's not the same as getting a call saying, "Sorry, you didn't get it." The opportunity just vanished.

From that point forward I made myself unavailable for interviews. I spent my days going to Theatre 80 on St. Marks Place, an old revival house that smelled like exterminator. I watched double features of the films of George Cukor, or Preston Sturges, or Woody Allen, or silent films. The bill changed every day, so it worked really well. I walked down from my apartment on Eightieth Street, picked up a sandwich from the 2nd Avenue Deli (turkey with Russian dressing), and sat in the dark, eating and watching. I dressed like an old Maine fisherman, in an oversized barn jacket with stay-dry pockets, and walked everywhere with my headphones, listening to Howard Stern on the radio and laughing out loud. At least I didn't have to worry about getting hit on.

While I waited for the movies to begin, I would write in a notebook. Short stories about tortured angsty girls at a variety of ages, all painfully beautiful but totally cuckoo, not washing their hair, peeing in their Chanel suits. One of the pieces won me acceptance into a well-known author's writing workshop at the 92nd Street Y. Only eighteen out of 150 applicants made it in. I always thought being a writer was a good idea because anytime anyone asked you what you were doing you could say, "I'm at work on a novel."

Oh, what's it about? Then, just a discreet finger across the lip, *Shhh . . . we musn't say any more.*

I was still sending out résumés that might as well have been rolled up inside bottles. As the buds appeared on the branches and the crocuses signified the approaching tanning season, I figured I'd take some time off from my grueling search and start back up in the fall.

All the while, my father had been trying to remove me from the dole, but like persistent dandruff, no amount of head scratching could shake me. Finally, he snapped.

"I have a surprise for you," he said on speakerphone one day while I was eating a bowl of Grape-Nuts and watching *Regis and Kathie Lee.*

"You bought me a car?" I said. "You're sending me to Europe?" My dad and I shared a lot of witty repartee about my being unemployed. When he took me to get my own American Express card before a trip to L.A. and the clerk asked me my occupation, he said, "Parasite." When we both looked at him, stunned, he added, "Like from Paris." Oh, the hilarity. The never-ending laughs were about to end.

"Julie, honey, I got you a job." Here is where I started to black out. What kind of job can you get for someone else? A job making Dilly bars at Dairy Queen? Running numbers? No, worse. I was to go to work in my dad's office. The insurance company. I would be a policy owner's service clerk. It would just be temporary, part-time, but enough hours to get benefits.

My nameplate should have said "I'm Leaving Soon," because that's all I ever said to anyone. Someone like me who watches so many movies should know not to say that kind of thing; it begs for a "Cut to: Retirement Ceremony—35 Years Later."

I started working there and soothed myself with the fact that Franz Kafka had been an insurance clerk. Although I knew I was more likely to turn into a giant cockroach than into Franz Kafka. Wallace Stevens was also very successful in the insurance game. I wasn't going to become him, either. Twenty-five hours a week brought me a whopping $324.76 every Friday.

I made friends with the unlikely group that was the office staff, four warm and lovely West Indian women who brought curried goat and blood pudding for lunch, and one middle-aged Italian gent who lived with his mother in a pink two-family home in Bensonhurst and was the owner of an impressive porcelain clown collection. This was where I was comfortable.

I'd come to the office with my dad my whole life. I could barely reach the giant mimeograph machine when I fell in love with the place. After lunching at Kaplan's at the Delmonico, where we had corned-beef sandwiches with Russian dressing under the orange lights, we'd head over to Butterfly chocolates for a double-dip cone. It was the 1970s, and there was no place I would rather be. New York was at its mid-Koch dirty best. And my father's office was heaven, gloriously carpeted in plush brown wall-to-wall, bedecked with chrome-and-leather furniture, with the air-conditioning blasting. I loved the city and his huge corner office overlooking Madison Avenue. He had a microcassette recorder that he used to dictate letters, and which I in turn would use to narrate what I saw out the window. My father would play the recordings later at dinner and we'd all get big laughs out of my attempt to pronounce the word "bureau." I visited with the glamorous borough secretaries, their desk radios playing "Native New Yorker," in their pleather stiletto heels, heaps of purple eye makeup, and talk of the best discos; they chain-smoked, dialed the phone with a pencil, read Dewar's (pronounced do-ers) profiles, and let me push the buttons on the elevators. After a day at my dad's office I tsawked in a Bvooklyn accent, droyving my bruddas cvazy.

I loved New York City, and the seventies was our golden time together. Love for the city is in my bones, but I got a push after a disastrous family trip out West. When I was ten, my dad chose a two-week summer vacation to the Grand Canyon, not to see the Grand Canyon, but to hike down it, then back up. So I didn't take gym, but I was being asked to hike 15.7 miles in 115-degree heat one day, and to repeat it the next day *uphill*. It was a huge flop. About midway down we bumped into a goofy guy who we all made fun of. He looked at us (me) skeptically and warned us to watch out for the Hazardous H's: hyponatremia (a.k.a. "water intoxication"), heatstroke, heat prostration, and hypothermia. The good news was, I didn't get hypothermia. The bad news was that I got so sick I barely knew where I was, and we were still far from the campsite. Somehow, though, I made it there and ate dinner and went to sleep. The plan was to get up before the sun, at four a.m., and begin the return trip. We left the air-conditioned cabin at a few minutes after four, and though the canyon was dark, it was already an oven. But unlike during the light of day, it was swarming with thousands of low-flying bats. Miles below the earth's surface, hot as a motherfucker, bats. My father was walking up ahead, and I looked to see if he'd grown a forked tail and cloven hooves, because this was most certainly hell.

Fortune struck again: I started puking and passing out, and the gods of the air came to our rescue. A large yellow-and-black helicopter lifted us to the surface in less than a few minutes. Matt and Brian were mad and embarrassed. Not me. We were in our hotel room that night, everyone's bodies aching. I saw a package of peanut M&M's in a pile with the wallet and change and ChapStick on my father's nightstand. "What is that?" I asked my mother.

"I don't know," she said.

We knew what M&M's were, but my father was a big health-food freak and he would sooner have purchased LSD than candy. He had bought them in the canyon snack shop in case I got weak on the hike up. This was the moment I was struck with the seriousness of what happened. My dad bought M&M's. He must have thought I was going to die.

"Can I eat them now?" I asked him.

"No," he said, chucking them in the trash.

I was safe.

The rest of the trip I sang "New York, New York" at the top of my lungs wherever we went.

. . .

New York while I was working in my father's office was a different story. My friends had good jobs at high-profile places, while I sank deeper and deeper into the low-pile carpets. Not being challenged or yelled at and getting home by four-thirty were very appealing to me. The people coming by my desk and saying "Still here?" were not. My dad's cronies would slip me information about "real jobs" I could apply for. I would tack them up on my cubicle, wait an appropriate amount of time, and then chuck them.

I talked a lot in therapy about how embarrassed I was about my job, but Margot correctly felt it was a very important experience for me to just have a job and get experience "showing up," after a lifetime of ADD—attendance deficit disorder.

It was a funny thing, but because I was always conscious when I was younger of other kids being jealous of me because of the number of Ralph Lauren sweaters I had or the horses or the tennis court, I had become the most self-deprecating teen on the planet. I'd boast about my failures. Who needs a pool? I CAN'T SWIM! You're jealous of my raspberry cashmere sweater? I know, I know, it highlights my acne.

It turned out, though, that I ended up being jealous of my friends with fully developed life skills. I had lunch with one woman I'd grown up with. She was working in a PR firm and she had to leave early that day to be home because her wall-to-wall carpeting was being installed. Oh, how I thought about her wall-to-wall carpeting. Fuck hardwood floors; they're cold. And she didn't have to ask anyone; she just did it. I wanted a dog for two years before I got one because I didn't really feel like I was allowed to have one. Since I wasn't supporting myself, everything went through the committee of my parents. The one very major breakthrough in that period was when my parents asked me for the eight-millionth time when I was going to be done with therapy. It was their right to ask. They were paying for it. I was so upset about it, but until Margot suggested it, it never occurred to me that I could pay for it myself. So I started doing that, and it was profoundly liberating (probably less so for Margot, who had to suffer through years of late payments from me). And to answer the question about when I'd be done with therapy, all I could say was, when I run out of problems, or die, whichever comes first.

EVERY MORNING I got to the insurance job and called my mother, according to phone records that were later brought to my attention, and spoke anywhere from forty-seven to eighty-five minutes without a break. It was important stuff, too. My mother had this compulsion to reenact one-hour television dramas from the night before. I'd sit there listening to her recount a full episode of *NYPD Blue*, complete with her crying during the emotional parts. The Dennis Franz character particularly moved her. It drove me crazy, because I didn't watch the show and didn't know the characters, but at the same time it fascinated me that this didn't seem to impede her.

"Mom, I need to at least look like I'm working."

"It's almost over!" she pleaded.

"I think we need to go to commercial break."

"You mean you don't want to hear how we saw Sipowitz's tushy?" she said, taunting.

"Yeah?" I said. She got me. "How'd it look?"

"Not bad," she said. I heard her pouring herself more coffee. "I've seen worse."

THE CALENDAR PAGES flew off as in a 1930s movie, with me superimposed in my Easter bonnet, carving a pumpkin, hanging garlands on the tree, and during that time my expertise in term, life, and disability insurance flourished. I had a new customer-servicey phone voice and knew just the right thing to say when an elderly woman called to report her husband's passing. "Oh, Mrs. Bloom, I am so very sorry for the loss of your loved one. I will do everything I can to expedite the claim and get your check out to you. Are you okay to talk now? Because I am going to need a little information." Some of these people were remarkably together. Others were heartbreakingly scattered. Especially the ones who dug up the policy while cleaning out their husband's papers, unaware that it had been cashed in years before and there was nothing left.

A pleasingly bucolic early spring morning found me walking to work, on my usual route, going north around the park before walking south on Fifth Avenue. I was listening on my Walkman to a cassette of songs I loved that I had taped off the radio (it was missing all the beginnings of the songs). I looked up at a tree near the entrance near to the Metropolitan Museum of Art. Small buds were just emerging. New life. Hope. But not for me. "It isn't all going to work out," I thought. And like that, with the snap of a twig, I was depressed.

Three weeks into it—after having my first I don't want to say suicidal thoughts, because it was more like thoughts about having suicidal thoughts—I'd had enough. I got on some good drugs, and it helped. But my sense of well-being was ruptured; I knew this thing was inside me somewhere, and I didn't want to see it again.

Toward the end of my sixth year at Berkshire Life, I went in to see my supervisor, Ms. Penny, for my performance evaluation. I was nodding my head and listening to her talk about the changes that she was looking forward to implementing in the coming year, desktop publishing of insurance materials and getting the office on e-mail. I watched out her windows as workers disassembled an *English Patient* billboard over Times Square and stifled my usual urge to push open the windows and leap out. I had just finished writing a movie script and had high hopes for it. But let's face it, those billboard guys were closer to being in the film business than I was.

Ms. Penny handed me a plastic sealed packet with a Berkshire Life Insurance key chain inside. I'd earned it for being with the company for six years. Rather than take the bauble and use it to slice my throat, I turned in my resignation. It was time.

At my surprisingly tearful going-away party I went back to my desk to check my home messages. Matt had sent my script to his agent, who sent it out to some Hollywood people. There was a message from the agent: apparently they thought it was good enough to give to the actress of the moment, and her people told the agent that it was the only script that had come in that everyone in the office unanimously loved.

I went back into the party smiling, knowing that this was my sign. I'd done the right thing.

For a few weeks I was Erich von Stroheim, walking around the Upper West Side telling Otto, "Someday all of this will be ours." I imagined my screenwriting millions and me back at the Letterman show, this time as a guest. I often imagined myself as his guest, even though I couldn't recall ever seeing other insurance clerks or screenwriters on his show.

The agent called me again; the people wanted me to do a rewrite of the star's next movie. She called me again. I was actually on the short list of writers to do the rewrite of the star's next movie. I started imagining my life in the booming voice of a 1930s newsreel. "With barely anything in her pocket to keep the lint and wadded-up tissue company, screenwriting hopeful Julie Klam went to Hollywood . . . and received the largest spec script sale on record, to the tune of $1,000,000,000,000,000 and back-end points!"

Fade to the week after, when probably-definitely went from looks-like-it to let-me-call-you-back to no one taking my call.

I sat with Otto in front of the Museum of Natural History, by the feet of Theodore Roosevelt, trying to figure out what had just happened. As the sun set and the sky turned into the majestic purple that only city lights and pollution can create, I reminded myself that you couldn't lose what you never had.

Otto, Mr. Live-in-the-Moment, pawed at my jeans and yawned. We may have been unemployed, but, he reminded me, we still had to eat. I picked up his leash and we walked home for dinner.

Four

Goodfellas Make Bad Bedfellas

AT THE MOMENTS when life has asked me to step up to the plate, I do what I did on the Katonah Cardinals in fourth grade: back way the hell away from any potential speeding balls that could hit me in the eye or face. I practiced avoidance. My teammates on the Cardinals begged me to stand there and get hit by the ball so I could get on base. It was the perfect plan: stay still, get hit, walk to first. Except I didn't want to get whacked by a hardball. But as anyone who's ever played Little League can tell you, the pitchers don't exactly have the control of a Catfish Hunter. I got hit and I got on base and that was the only way I ever scored in a game. Twenty years later I was still backing away. I found the death of my grandfather and the burgeoning awareness that

I was not where I should be overwhelming enough to keep me hidden beneath videos, takeout, and my dog for the rest of my life. Then I got hit.

It was at the dog run near the Hayden Planetarium construction site that Gentleman Joe found his opening with me. I was staring at Otto running back and forth, jealous of his single-mindedness, when a husky voice startled me out of my reverie.

"What type of dog is that, miss?"

"Boston terrier," I said. I worried that I was getting in trouble.

He was a construction worker who was flagging the cement trucks into the museum's driveway, and I had noticed him before. He reminded me of Colin Farrell or Benicio Del Toro—dark, a resting facial expression that was sexy and dodgy and a little pissed off, with the kind of muscles you get from working, not working out.

He asked me what I did for a living, why I was around all day, because, you see, he had noticed me, too. He said he always noticed beautiful women.

"I'm a writer," I announced, defensively zooming in on the part about me being around all day, not the beautiful part.

"A writer?" He responded as if I had said I was a rocket scientist or a brain surgeon. "Wow, a real writer!"

Then he asked me to lunch. I said no. Who doesn't know that you're supposed to ignore come-ons from construction workers? A couple of days later I ran into him again. He was leaning against the wall of a deli near my apartment, eating macaroni salad with a plastic fork. He dumped the half-full container into the trash and said, "I'm taking you to lunch." He swept me into a booth at Ray's Original Pizza.

The first meal we shared together, Joe paid. I remember it like yesterday. He boasted that girls didn't pay when they were out with him. I was so impressed. He was not like the guys I normally dated, the anemic-looking office workers—men who made six figures but didn't want to pay for your glass of seltzer until they knew it might be going somewhere. I ordered a slice, plain, and bottled water.

I started interviewing him the minute we sat down. First question, how old was he? Thirty-eight. Where was he from? Born and bred in Brooklyn, the GREATEST BOROUGH IN THE WORLD! How long had he been doing construction? Only about two years. Before that he had been away. He looked at me to see if I got his meaning. I did not. Away to me meant the Riviera or Southampton. Away to him meant something else entirely. Jail. Federal penitentiaries. A bunch of them. He stared at me hard to see if I was going to jump up and run off. On the contrary, this was the movie I'd been waiting to see. I asked him with great delicacy if he could tell me why. No hesitation—armed robbery and racketeering. He said it was an honest mistake. "I took withdrawals from banks that I didn't have accounts at." Ha ha ha. There was nothing remotely resembling shame in this. I thought he was bravely honest, but he just didn't give a shit about it. He was proud that he kept his mouth shut and took his lumps; it was the first time he'd mention *omertà*, the Mafia term referring to not ratting on anyone. So he was a wiseguy, too? No, no. He was at best an "associate" of the

Gambino family. Did he ever meet John Gotti? Sure, John gave him a boost when he got out of prison . . . the first time.

All told he had been incarcerated for fifteen years; he said he'd been away so long his clothes were back in style. The only regret he had about his crime was that he'd been "pinched." What, he wondered, was the difference between a shylock lending money at five points and Citibank lending money at twenty percent? Banks loan money and it's legal; a shylock does it and he gets hauled in for loan-sharking and extortion. Well, I suggested, Citibank typically did not break your legs if you were late paying. But, he countered, they took your house. Which was worse, really?

"Use ya head!" he said, and it kind of made sense.

I wondered why he was so comfortable telling me this stuff, sitting here in the middle of a busy pizzeria. He said he didn't worry because we didn't run in the same circles and I didn't seem like I had a big mouth. He told me he thought I'd find the story interesting and maybe I could even write about him. Hmmm. Yes, writing. That *was* what I was supposed to be doing, but when it came right down to it, I didn't really know what to write about. I had the beginnings of a dozen stories. I had that feeling that I had in elementary school when there was a jump-rope game on the playground. The really good jump-ropers would walk up to the spinning rope, sort of rocking back and forth with their hands up to get the rhythm, and then jump in. "A, my name is Aynsley." When I went, I stood and did the readying, but as far as I remember, the rope was still waiting for me when the sun set. If I got the courage to jump in, the rope got caught on my foot. "We're not jump-ropers!" my mother said. We're not much of anything, I was starting to think.

After agreeing to eat lunch again the next day, I went home and started looking him up on the Internet. Joseph Vincent Caputo and seven other guys with Italian names were convicted in 1980 of the armed robbery of twenty-nine banks in Manhattan, Brooklyn, and Staten Island in 1979, and were suspected of many more. According to *The New York Times*, he and his associates were caught when a "joint bank robbery task force was set up by the FBI and NYPD after a jump in such crimes." When I looked further I found dozens of articles about New York's bank robbery crime wave of 1979. There was a quote from then mayor Ed Koch announcing spectacularly to all the robbers at large: "Remember what happened to Dillinger! He was shot!" In New York City that year there had been a virtual epidemic of bank heists, with more than 450 reported through July—a record 125 in July alone. One day in August, fourteen banks were held up, and the next day's *New York Post* headline spouted "The Day the Hoods Ran New York." And on and on. I was so excited to meet Joe the next day to get more of his story. I had the feeling you get in high school when you look forward to seeing your crush at his locker. It was like someone had injected me with adrenaline.

Back at Ray's, with his orange construction helmet on the table beside him, he demonstrated how he tied a bandanna around his nose and mouth, then took my baseball cap and put it on his head backward. The only thing missing was his mirrored aviator Ray-Bans. He acted out a holdup, then went on to tell me that the only day his inspired disguise failed him was when he robbed the Franklin Savings Bank in Staten Island and his aunt was in there making a deposit for her boss. She recognized him, and when she saw him the following Sunday at supper she smacked him in the head. He promised her he wouldn't do it again.

I wanted to know how he got caught. He very bluntly explained that one of the guys in his gang was a drug user and he gave the others up when he was picked up for dealing PCP. ("Oh, he sang?" I said. "People don't say that no more, Julie.") He wanted me to know the guy was no longer operating, as in alive. End of story.

He told me everything about himself, or everything he wanted me to know. He was living with his mother, sort of . . . had a crazy ex-girlfriend somewhere, very sketchy on the details. During the stories he interjected little things about me. "My best friend's uncle was Joe Colombo—you know you got a great ass, Klam—I was away with the guy who *Dog Day Afternoon* was based on. Yeah, he used to walk around with a toy doll—you ever wear your hair up?—I'd tell the guards, 'Hey, come here, nice shirt, you wanna open this door?' . . . [*Laughs*] You are beautiful, I know you don't know that." I'll admit it, I was thrilled. There was none of that sort of thing where I was trying to read him, see if he liked me, wondering if he'd call. We continued to meet for lunches, and he'd always start with, "Go ahead, ask me anything."

There were no dates set up. His nights were off limits, for now anyway. And before you start wondering, sure, the voices in my head said, "Bad idea," but I told them to keep quiet.

The weekend after I met Joe, my father's father died. He had been an orphan in the New York of the early 1900s. In and out of juvenile hall, he'd run numbers, bootlegged, anything he could do to make a buck for his family. He eventually chose to change his name and go straight—I think when he met my grandmother. I remember one time when Matt and I got in a car accident; Matt was a junior in high school and I was in ninth grade. He made me steer the wheel of our Scout Traveler (I didn't want to) and we ended up in a ravine. My grandfather, who'd been staying with us while our parents were in Spain, got to the accident scene and said, "Don't tell the cops anything!" Maybe the loss of my grandfather made Joe more attractive to me at the time. Or the fact that I was so desperately in need of some genuine life experience. All I know is that one day I felt like I had no life and the next day I fancied myself a sort of wannabe Bonnie Parker. I kept telling myself it was just temporary, lunches, a little messing around behind the museum. It provided great stories and great research for something I would eventually write about.

About three weeks after we met, at eleven o'clock on a Thursday night, my front-door buzzer woke me up. It was Joe with his cousin Frank (one of fifty men named Frank I met through him). This Frank was about six-foot-five and was obsessed with how I was able to clean the moldings of the twenty-foot ceilings in my apartment. (I didn't.)

Joe, it seemed, had gotten into a big fight with his

stepfather, Sal, that fat fuck, and he wanted to know if he could crash at my place. In my bones, I knew this was the absolute wrong thing to do and I said so. A month before, I was planning to retire at Woodmont. I was scared. Until now the romance was like a game, cops and robbers, maybe, or writers and robbers. I had seen him only in the safety of daylight. I told him he could stay the night but then he absolutely had to find somewhere else to go. He said he would. The cousin came back in from his car with two garbage bags of clothes and a shoe box of photos, told me I was "good people," and left. Then we talked, I mean really talked. The fight with his stepfather was about borrowing money from his mother to pay back an "underboss" he owed. He was starting to panic, visibly. He just needed to give the guy $3,000, and he'd be able to get back into some action to make some real money. If I could lend it to him, he'd sign a note saying he owed it to me plus twenty percent interest, and he'd have it to me within two months, or eight weeks, whichever I preferred (he tried to sound lawyerly, inserting "in which" into his sentences, as in "In which I will return to you your loan"). Plus—and this was where it got interesting—he was going to give me a $500 gift certificate to Bergdorf Goodman. It sounded like a really good deal; my pea brain thought I might actually make money. He seemed much more vulnerable than he had before and I think that was what ultimately made me say that I'd help him. I regretted it even as the words passed my teeth. Three thousand dollars. A third of the savings I had from a small inheritance. I was cautious, I lived within my means, I always paid my bills on time, and I was really hoping I'd get my $3,000 back.

Lots of people see red flags when they get into relationships. I know people who have started dating men and worried they were married to their jobs or womanizers or lived too far away. At the same time I met Joe, my two best friends were starting equally unclear relationships. One was blithely ignoring the fact that her new guy was a cokehead. The other's new boyfriend wasn't quite finished with his ex-girlfriend; he really liked my friend, and things with the ex had been sour for a while, but they'd been together for eight years and he was just not letting go. We probably all thought the other ones were putting on blinders going into these relationships. But sometimes you just have to see where it will go. Sometimes things work out. Sometimes they don't.

Joe left early the next morning, after about a ninety-minute shower (he was very, very clean), to see if he could find a place to stay. Everyone he asked said it was a bad time, but maybe they could help him out soon. If he could just leave his stuff at my place he would stay out of my way. My place was a studio apartment; air was in my way.

Joe was very candid about the mess he had made of his life. He returned the next night and over more pizza gave me his take on how his life got so screwed up. First, his father died when he was eleven ("done in by a bum ticker"), then his best friend, the guy he idolized for being able to shake down any business, was killed in a motorcycle accident. He did poorly in school, and it "turned to shit" from there. He fumed about his ex-girlfriend, "the crack haw."

He had a kid with her, but she had "stolen him away" and taken him to "parts unknown"—maybe Georgia; she had a sister down there. He cried about missing his son, and wondered if he'd ever find him. He never imagined this was where his life would lead: a high school dropout, homeless, broke, a record as long as your arm. When he was young he had wanted to be a professional baseball player. His coach thought he could have been the next Mel Stottlemyre.

Around three in the morning he got to the part about the nervous breakdown he'd suffered a month before he was released from jail. He heard voices in his head. Every day he would call his old friend Gina, a sweet, chubby New York City bus driver I met a few times, and she would ask to speak to these voices. She would say, "Hey, you voices, listen to me. You get outta Joe's head!" I told him it sounded to me like he had been afraid to go back to the real world, especially since shortly after he was released, he violated parole (he was part of a crew conspiring to rob the guy from Zabar's who took the cash to the bank at the end of the day—"It was just a kid on a bike!"). They locked him up for five more years; he got out again and violated again. He disagreed with my diagnosis. He told me he wanted to be out of there so bad he had even chosen to work in the jail kitchen because the apples he touched came from the outside. I began filling a notebook with his quotes.

We talked a lot those first few nights. He was still haunted by his demons; he had been in prison almost as long as he'd been out. He had routines in jail (he called them "rituals"), but was uncomfortable in civilian life. He told me that when he got to a new prison (they move inmates around with some regularity to keep them from getting too connected at one facility), he would be shown to his cell and request a bucket and ammonia and scrub the cell till his fingers bled. Every inch. Another friend of his who'd been away whom I met, Nicky, said he did the same thing. They were criminals, but they were not immune to cooties.

I THINK SOMEHOW I thought of him as developmentally disabled. A project to focus on. He went to jail at nineteen and got out for good at thirty-six. He was, in many respects, still a teenager. I guess I saw myself the same way. He'd been in jail during the prom; I was home watching *The French Connection*. Around him I didn't feel like a relationship freak because of my having so little prior experience; quite the contrary. He once announced that he and I weren't "boyfriend and girlfriend" yet because he hadn't "asked me out," like, to go steady. I informed him that that was not how adults became a couple. He was quite shocked.

Imagine me, the expert. My prior history could not have filled a Post-it. What I was most talented at was smoke and mirrors. I dated a lot, but my longest relationship was three months, and the guy was away for a month of that time—really away, in Brazil, not in jail.

It was a primary focus in therapy: What exactly was wrong with me? I didn't like anyone very much, I wasn't comfortable. Someone would ask me for my number, or I'd get set up. A week before the date I'd start preparing: facials, extra workouts, and not eating. By the time the date rolled around I'd be tired, dizzy, and resentful. Inside my head the thoughts went something like this: "I spent forty hours preparing for this date, bought a new camisole, lost five pounds, and stuffed my horrendously disfigured bunioned feet into cute boots. And you couldn't get the long hair out of your nose?" I thought of myself as being a great charmer, because I knew what most people liked to yammer on about: themselves.

At the end of the night, I'd be fed up. I wanted to go home and have a bowl of cereal and get the tight jeans and boots off. Never again, I'd think as I ate my granola with Otto beside me. He heartily agreed. Dating took me away from him and occasionally knocked him out of the bed. The team (my mother and friends) would call the next day and see how it went, and I would tell them the guy was a self-centered jerk and he had a hair in his nose that was so long he could've used it to floss his teeth.

JOE NEVER MISSED a fireworks display; he said it helped replace the "jail paint" in his mind. He said when he first got sent away his mind was filled with the outside and little by little jail had painted over it till the memories all came from there. His holiday recollections were all from the can. He told me he wished he could just tilt his head and let those images fall out his ear.

He needed me, and I was sure I could help him. That was what I did. I started calling around about GED exams, asking my parents' friend who owned a construction company if there was anything he could do for Joe (who was now finished with the Planetarium job), and started researching child-locator services. I wanted him to go into therapy. Slowly I began to get comfortable with him. There was something irresistible and charming about the fact that he seemed frozen in time. He was a powder-blue Pan Am bag, Al Pacino, and the Brothers Johnson's "Stomp." He was New York in the seventies.

He would never use my phone—only pay phones, so he couldn't be tracked. Mystery and paranoia surrounded everything. He came and went from my place but wasn't "living" there . . . just his stuff was. I rifled through his photos, and they backed up everything he said. There he was in the yard at Otisville, sitting around with a crew of tracksuit-clad *paesans*, and here were the son and the crazy ex-girlfriend at the South Street Seaport. Little Joe was a carbon copy of Joe. Donna was a Puerto Rican knockout, despite the huge hair, bad home highlights, and piles of makeup; she was dressed in her best white shoulder-padded, stud-laden suit and hooker pumps. I was interested in her, having heard countless stories of how evil she was (this I knew to take with a grain of salt). I learned about the many times she went nuts (unprovoked, of course) on Joe, knocking him out with a frying pan, calling the cops on him, dialing all the numbers on his beeper, hiding out in wait for him all night, setting his car on fire. She was "the jealous type," and a drug user who had five other kids with four other guys. This was the woman he belonged with, not me. I got very creeped out when I started to relate to her.

As much as I had made the rule that he couldn't hang out at my apartment, his disappearances for days at a time still made me crazy. He didn't answer his beeper, even when I typed my number and 911, the code for "emergency" that people with beepers use. He used to turn it off or throw it out windows. Where did he go? "The less you know the better, Jules, trust me." I, of course, assumed it was not an illegal venture but another girl.

I was constantly telling myself that I wasn't being used, that he meant everything he said. Even if he couldn't follow through on it, at least he believed he could. It became a given that I would pay for everything—his meals, his MetroCards, his clothes, some new Mephisto shoes, plus the inevitable "walkin' around money." We both kept track of it all in a composition notebook, the idea being that he would pay back every cent plus interest when he could. He had a lot of plans that he seemed sure were going to pan out, and a lot of lotto tickets. I started to get terrible insomnia and would find myself up at three a.m., studying my bank balance and credit-card statements. Never before had I just paid the monthly minimums. Trying to stop the runaway train, I began temping. It really pissed me off that I was trying to figure out ways to pay the bills while Joe sat on his ass, waiting for his numbers to hit. Every so often he visited the cement laborers' union to flirt with the girls there and check for jobs. He'd get a day here or two days there. It was a slow time. Things would pick up. I was definitely enabling him, in collusion with his schemes; I was in his bubble.

One of Joe's major problems was that he didn't have a

car. If he just had a car . . . (fill in the million things that he would do). He could never accept any of the big money-making jobs his friends offered him because he didn't have wheels. There was a narcoleptic capo in Brooklyn who could use him for driving and odd jobs, but not with no car. He could "collect vig" for the acting boss of the Bonanno family, *if* he had a car. It was all I heard from him. Then one day, the Bonanno guy said he'd give him the money for a used car if he'd do something for him; the problem was he couldn't register the car in his own name for reasons having to do with the crazy ex blowing up his old car. He immediately told me that he would not let me put it in my name! He would not hear of it! (This was a classic move; he would not allow me to do X, until somehow I was begging him to let me.) So off we went to downtown Brooklyn, to Cholly Parmegianni the insurance guy, and suddenly my name was on that stupid fucking ice-blue pearl Crown Vic. The Ford Crown Victoria. The same car cops drive, the car that has the same chassis as a Lincoln. The minute I signed the paper I felt the familiar thunk in my gut that I got when I lent him money. After seeing the despair on my face, he decided to take me out in the new old car, Joe style! We'd forget our troubles and have a fabulous dinner at Marco Polo's and go parking under the Verrazano Bridge. Yeah, I paid.

It was a crystal-clear night and the bridge was lit up like a tiara. Romance was in the air as Joe completely flipped out over the fact that the glove compartment would not stay closed, stupid-fuckin'-rat-motherfuckin'-used-car-piece-of-shit. Then it was all about how he could never have a new car. Poor him. Slamming the glove compartment again and again and again. I said, "That's good, I'm sure it's fixed now."

The temper tantrums didn't faze me; my dad used to flip out on inanimate objects. I just waited it out. Then, like a switch, he turned it off and he was back to his charismatic self. He was at times hysterically funny, and always an animated and terrific storyteller—a mix of racketeer and raconteur. He offered to set up my dear friend Barbara, who had just broken up with her boyfriend, with someone from a good family. And she could choose, too—Lucchese, Gambino, Genovese, Bonanno, or Colombo. When Shari Lewis died, he wanted us to have lamb chops for dinner, as a tribute. He told me about the first crimes he and his friends committed, at age twelve: stealing the cars of wiseguys on Friday nights. A Lucchese capo who looked after him when his father died called him to the club on a Saturday afternoon and scared the shit out of him.

"Look, you gotta stop doin' this. Friday night these big gangsters, made guys, are out on dates, they come out of a nice restaurant and their cars are gone! They're ridin' the bus home! It don't look good! You gotta steal from somebody else." The captain suggested an area where he would find nice cars and no trouble, and then gave him ten bucks to go get a lemon ice.

He introduced me to his friends, high-ups in La Cosa Nostra. Some owned four-star restaurants in midtown; others were splashed across the front page of the *Post* on a regular basis. There was Fat Stevie, Fat Richie, Fat

Carmine, and a guy who Joe told me looked just like "the turtle in Pinocchio." (He meant Jiminy Cricket.) I remember meeting another guy who I was told was "half a fag, but he beat it—went out, got married, had kids." Fixing homosexuality was a big thing with him. Joe was furious and disappointed that neither his gay brother nor his lesbian sister put any effort into correcting their situations.

He liked to know what was in the papers but didn't want to read them. "Anybody I know in there?" I'd tell him all the organized-crime-related news. He said in jail they'd bring around a cart with old newspapers, magazines, books without covers. He read the biography of Princess Grace, though. Twice.

We spent some strange days together. One day I found myself setting up a nursery for the fat narcoleptic wiseguy's Russian girlfriend, who was expecting his kid. Another time I was told to wait on a park bench for Joe while he got into a dark-windowed Mercedes, and not to look at him when he got out of the car, and not to look his way at all until the Mercedes was out of sight. I definitely felt like I was in a movie, but some days it was *GoodFellas*, and others it was *9½ Weeks*.

He was smart, even though he said "Floridian slip" instead of "Freudian slip." There were only a few times when I was with him when I thought I might eventually get bored. Once when I watched him sitting at my coffee table surrounded by lotto tickets, trying to figure out every combination of lotto numbers. When I looked, he had fifty cards filled out with all number ones and was starting on the next set with the number two. He still hadn't figured out what to fill in the other slots. My head was spinning. Someone at the pork store (Brooklynese for Italian deli) had a friend whose cousin had just won $46,000. He figured with roughly a $200 investment he would definitely hit the big number . . . or at least something.

Another time he wanted me to time him eating hot dogs because he was sure he could win the hot-dog-eating contest on Coney Island. One of my least favorite images of myself during this relationship is the one of me standing by a hot dog cart in Central Park, looking at my watch while he shoved hot dog after hot dog down his throat to prove he could beat the "Chinese kid" who won. ("And this is me eatin' leisurely!") He considered it a blight against Brooklyn that a neighborhood guy couldn't win the Nathan's Famous Hot Dog Eating Contest.

He continued to come and go, always with a bang. He'd check in with me, always sensing when I was starting to drift, when he might be losing me. Then he'd pull something, or someone, out of his hat. Once he took me on a very emotional tour of Green-Wood Cemetery in Brooklyn. He showed me where his best friend and his grandmother were buried. The grandmother once took a bus from Elizabeth Street in Little Italy into Brooklyn to smack his father with a rolling pin (she brought the rolling pin with her) for hitting his mother. He also tried to find the grave of a woman who had died in the bathtub, her gravestone supposedly an actual bathtub. We never found it.

Joe's mantra when I got upset was "One day you can write about it." That and "I'm *gonna* pay you back."

There were more tours of the Brooklyn you can't see unless you're a part of it: Here is where Son of Sam shot Stacy Moskowitz and Robert Violante in 1977. Here's where this wiseguy threw that wiseguy into a woodchipper. Here are the insane animatronic Christmas lights of Dyker Heights, and the Italian-American kitchens. While he was away, he made his mother and all of her friends ceramic arts and crafts. Each kitchen we went into was graced with the kitty cat cookie jar, the Easter bunny basket, the banana canoe, and his scrawled signature.

On a particularly memorable evening we had dinner in Little Italy (It-ly)—my treat—and then went to the set of *Analyze This*, where his uncle was working. We chatted with Robert De Niro and Joe DiMaggio and then walked across the Brooklyn Bridge. That night we went back to my place. "Okay, everyone, back in your cells," he said as he opened my door. (He thought it was funny that I had bars on my windows to keep out criminals—"always with the bars on the windows.") He then went into the bathroom for a particularly long time. I thought it was the greasy dinner, but later he told me that he had been hiding guns in there. Oy. Friggin'. Vey.

I eventually started to get depressed; I didn't see any money coming in. Nothing ever happened that he said would happen. It didn't look good for me and I was scared about what I'd do and how I'd get out. Then he took me to meet his mother. "Would I take you to meet my mother if I wasn't going to pay you back? My *mother*?!"

We opened the door to her walk-up; she was standing at the top of the stairs with a dishtowel in her hand, looking dismayed. She had dyed red hair and tired eyes and wore a housecoat. She had just returned home from her job as a cook for a priest. She looked me up and down, me in my Burberry toggle coat and blond ponytail.

"So where'd you fall from?" Her gravelly voice and thick Brooklyn accent jolted me.

"Pardon me?" I said.

"WHERE DID YOU FALL FROM?" It was a well-put question, because I felt like a space alien. I told her the Upper West Side and was shot an angry look from Joe; he didn't like me to tell anyone where I lived because his crazy ex-girlfriend might track me down. His mother yelled at Joe to take his shoes off before stepping onto the spotless kitchen linoleum. I took my boots off and stared into the blinking eyes of a 3-D Jesus. In a not-too-hushed voice she asked, "What is she doing here?"

And that *was* the question, and still is the question. What *was* I doing there? I didn't belong there; I didn't belong with Joe. Still, his mother treated me well on this and future visits. His whole family acted like I was Lady Di. They all tried to speak correct English around me, saying things like "How did you find your cacciatore?" ("Whaddya mean?" Joe said, annoyed. "She looked down at her plate! That's how she found it!") They couldn't hide who they were, though. I remember cringing at one Caputo family dinner when the men were heatedly discussing what fucking scumbags the Kennedys were for their part in enacting the RICO laws.

My family, however, did not equally embrace him. They didn't so much hate him as, well, okay, they hated him.

Really, really hated him. It was hard to rebel against my parents growing up, but at age thirty, I did it.

Joe came with me to one Rosh Hashanah dinner at my aunt Mattie's on the Upper East Side. My brothers were amused by/scared of him. My father looked pained; my mother was trying to be supportive of me. There was one exchange between Joe and my dad. Joe was boasting that he had no tattoos or piercings, and my father was pointedly telling him about some guy in the NFL with dreadlocks and tattoos and piercings who had gone to Harvard and worked with kids and what a great guy he was. Joe had had one thing to offer and my father rejected it. That was pretty much it. All of my girl cousins clutched their purses when they were around him, and I overheard one of them say he was worse than Al, a legendary guy who had dated my uncle's second wife's daughter. He'd come to Thanksgiving years before, wearing a shirt that said GO FUCK YOURSELF, and talked at length about his hemorrhoids.

At dinner, Mattie was telling us all how much trouble she was having with the contractor who was redoing her deck in Montauk. Joe offered to "talk" to him. She nervously but politely declined. This was one of the worst days I ever had. I was furious that no one gave him a chance. In my view, he was trying to be a better person.

"How?" my mother wanted to know as we argued down the hallway from Mattie's apartment.

"None of your business," I said, defiantly.

My mother looked into my face, squinting her eyes, and said, "Are you in there?"

I felt like Regan in *The Exorcist*. Of course I thought I was in there, this was me, exactly who I was. My relatives looked at me like I was dancing around in a saffron robe with a shaved head. A few days later, I received a five-page handwritten letter from my father pleading with me to stop seeing Joe. He wrote: "I thought this whole thing was a joke. This is not what I want for you." I cried and cried like a misunderstood teenager; I was so mad at everyone for not seeing what I saw.

Brian sent an e-mail to all the kids in the family. He found a note he'd written about speaking to Grandpa Saul, and he wanted to share it with us.

> September 30, 1996
>
> I just got off the phone with Grandpa Saul, and I hope I never forget how it made me feel. . . . Grandpa said he's gonna play golf, read his books, go out with Ethel, play cards, and when someone taps him on the shoulder, he's gonna say fuck you, good-bye. "I've lived a good life, I had a wonderful marriage, great kids, and eleven wonderful grandchildren, all of whom I'm very proud. What more can I want? I've been very lucky. When I go, I want you to go out and have a big drink, because when I go, I'm gone and I'm not gonna miss it. When I go, I'm going in a blaze of glory."

"Eleven wonderful grandchildren, all of whom I'm very proud." Had he been proud of me? Would he be proud now?

Margot, whose policy it was not to judge, began to show

support for the situation. She said it was a necessary and healthy growth measure for me, as long as I wasn't in danger and we used condoms, and *as long as I wasn't lending him any money*. I told her I was paying for things here and there, sure. . . .

None of my friends ever came right out and told me they didn't like him. I wasn't being honest with myself, and I sure wasn't being honest with them. I was careful never to say anything that would reveal Joe's screwups. But they knew. I had a holiday party where several friends were going to meet him. He showed up at three in the morning, long after everyone had gone.

My feelings throughout had vacillated between anger, pity (for him, and then for myself), and confusion. Everything finally became clear on a Saturday afternoon in December. While I had been out getting a Christmas tree, Joe's mother had left several urgent messages for me on my machine. I beeped him and told him to call her. *Now.* Half an hour later, Joe stormed into my apartment with the news: authorities in Louisiana had arrested the crazy ex-girlfriend for heroin possession and put his kid in foster care. He was yelling and pounding the walls. Okay, here was the situation—he needed to get down to Louisiana and get his kid. Against Margot's fervent protests, I called Visa and had them FedEx me a new credit card with Joe's name on it. He used it to fly down to Baton Rouge, hire a lawyer, and bring home Little Joe. In less than four days he maxed out a ten-thousand-dollar credit card. It was the money I felt the least bad about losing. I picked Joe and his boy up at the airport.

There he was, with this lost-looking skinny child wearing glasses and a brand-new Mickey Mouse T-shirt. I remember wondering who got him his glasses. Was it Joe or the crazy ex or Joe's mother or the authorities?

In the brief time that Joe had been in Louisiana, he and his mother had made arrangements for some woman Joe had gone to grade school with to take him and the kid in. She had a whole floor in a two-family house in Red Hook. Apparently she'd always been in love with Joe. What was he supposed to do? It was over between us.

I looked up the definition of "psychopath" and it reads like a checklist of Joe's personality. Glibness/superficial charm, grandiosity, pathological lying, manipulative behavior, juvenile delinquency, accepting no responsibility for their actions, no ability to plan ahead, irresponsible, impulsive, etc. . . . Oh, and parasitic.

All of us in romantic entanglements take things from the other person against our will, without our knowledge—we take our partner's friends and work connections, we take our partner's way of talking and eating pizza, we take our partner's clothes, parents, music, ideas, or we borrow these things without asking. What Joe wanted from me was a cashier's check. And the truly shocking part came when I told my parents he was gone, expecting them to bail me out, and they didn't. I had made this bed and I was forced to sleep in it, alone.

Five

One of These Days I Gotta Get Myself Organizized

I HAD A PHOTOGRAPH that was taken of Joe in prison, out in the "yard," in 1982. His hair was combed back and he was wearing a tank top exploding with muscles. He was twenty-two. I stared at it, listening to Sarah McLachlan, weeping. My heart was broken. My jailbird boyfriend had dumped me for someone with a bigger apartment, and he had taken my $17,000. Even worse, those tears were the only thing that was real about the relationship. The memory of my post-Joe dramatics was so mortifying to me that when it was over, not only did I throw away every Sarah McLachlan CD of mine, I made Jancee throw out hers. Sarah had witnessed me in my lamest moment.

Somehow in the midst of it all, I had written a feature on

the sitcom *Frasier* for a magazine that seemed to have a ton of money but lasted about thirty seconds. They sent me for a photo shoot with a team of hair and makeup people for my contributor photo. It was freezing and bleak and I did not want to leave my apartment. I also do not like to have my picture taken, especially a head shot. When people want to take my picture I have them back up, back up, back up, until they end up with an aerial view of Manhattan. Now, that's a pretty picture.

The studio was at Chelsea Piers, overlooking the Hudson. The room was decorated in a funky industrial style, with bright white walls, and windows that let in the relentless sun. The team made me look very tan and blond and a fan was blowing warm air at my hair. Bang! I was Jennifer Aniston on the cover of *Bazaar.*

At age fifteen I had three favorite books: *Marjorie Morningstar*, *A Stone for Danny Fisher*, and a coffee-table book called *Scavullo Women*, by Francesco Scavullo, the *Cosmo* cover photographer. On my lime-green bedroom bookcase, the book was jammed between *Christie Brinkley's Outdoor Beauty and Fitness Book*, Cheryl Tiegs's *The Way to Natural Beauty*, and *The Ford Model's Crash Course in Looking Great.* I was a beauty-tip junkie and pored over the Scavullo photos of makeovers until the pages were faded. Most of the women didn't need makeovers—Brooke Shields, Donna Summer, Elizabeth Taylor, Gia (the model who died of AIDS), Patti Hansen, Rene Russo, Kim Alexis. Other subjects very much did. One of them was a young woman who looked like, and was, an overweight refugee from a New

Jersey high school, with bad highlights and frizzy, permed-out hair. Apparently, she was also wealthy enough to have a Scavullo photo shoot. Her "after" picture was stunning. In a black leather jacket, with wet hair and phenomenal makeup, she looked just like the models. The story that went with the picture said that she was so delighted by her "after" photos that she was inspired to make herself look that way in real life. She darkened her hair and cut out the perm, lost weight, and got a black leather jacket.

Toward the end of my shoot, I got a little less self-conscious and even laughed. (Though no amount of Madonna's "Ray of Light" could've gotten me to dance, as the photographer requested. Her assistant, though, was dancing enough for everyone.)

I took a Polaroid home of me looking like someone with a fabulous life: laughing, hand in my hair. I decided I would get my shit together and be that photo. A girl who'd have been worthy of my grandfather's pride.

A couple of days later, as the feelings of fabulosity were wearing off, like the color on the Polaroid, I was starting to feel like Miss Havisham from *Great Expectations* or Susan Alexander Kane from *Citizen Kane* or Mary Tyrone from *Long Day's Journey into Night*, my special movie idols who were all dressed up with no place to go but nuts.

Then the phone rang.

"Is Julie Klam there?"

"This is she."

"Oh, hi, this is Paul calling. I'm the producer of a show called *Pop-Up Video*."

"Hi!" My brain started working. I knew his name from his credit. I watched the show obsessively. It was an obscenely clever program that paired bubbles of info with music videos. I wondered if I had won a contest or if it was just someone messing with my head.

"I have your résumé here, I'm not sure how."

Two years earlier, I had been interviewed for a job on another show on VH1 and the woman who produced it offered to pass my résumé along to someone at *Pop-Up Video*. I'd forgotten about it until just now.

"Two years ago?" he said. "Well"—long pause—"how have you been?"

"Not so great. My boyfriend just dumped me." I thought about Jancee, who always said to me, *When people ask you how you are, they don't really want to know; just say fine.*

Paul paused again. "Well, he was an ass and he didn't deserve you."

I laughed. He sounded like a nice guy with a fresh-faced wife and two kids whose Little League teams he coached. He had a pleasant voice; I could see him clearly in my head. Bad haircut, little round glasses, pants belted too high.

"Are you still looking for a job?" he asked.

"Always," I said. He started describing the test I would need to take to get hired, and that's when I stopped listening. There were few things I was sure of, but one was that I Would Never Write for a Successful TV Show.

The next day a packet arrived in the mail with a video and instructions on how to "pop" it. This was the test. There were two *Pop-Up Video* stickers in there, too. I guess one was for my loose-leaf binder and the other for my locker. It was a Thursday and the test was due the following Friday. I put the whole envelope on top of my TV and forgot about it. Joe stopped by one day and asked about it and said, "Imagine that, I seen this show at the club on the TV and here it is in your house and you're actually going to work there."

"I didn't get the job yet."

"You will," he said, slipping his favorite CD in the player. He selected a song—it was Enya's "Sail Away." He discovered it on the Crystal Light iced tea commercial.

The day before my test script was due, I sent Paul an e-mail saying that I was going to be late because I had to go to L.A. for a meeting with Tom Cruise. That was a Julie-truth. The real story was that my screenplay had picked up some life and gone to Cruise/Wagner Productions. I asked if Monday would be okay and he said sure, but that I shouldn't let Tom become my rebound guy. I liked him. (Paul, not Tom Cruise.)

Sunday rolled around and I took the video out and watched it. It was the Wallflowers' "One Headlight." Pretty quickly my brain turned it into the two-trains-going-fifty-and-seventy-five-miles-per-hour essay question. But I felt that having said I would do it, I should. My brother knew someone who had worked on the show. He told me that Paul loved puns (he didn't) and that a pop should come every seven seconds (not necessarily). So I began, and in a couple of hours I had a finished script. For better or worse.

The next day I decided to drop the script off at Paul's office with the receptionist. I wanted to go by Joe's construction site first and see if he had any money for me. I had a cab wait for me, and Joe decided to get in and come with me.

There was no receptionist out front, but there was a massive tank of bubbles. Betsy, the woman I had met from the VH1 show two years before, was walking by. We exchanged pleasantries and I asked her where I could drop the script.

"Well, Paul's here. You can give it to him."

I pointed a finger in Joe's face and through clenched teeth said, "Stay here, I'm not kidding." Betsy took me back into the offices.

Paul was standing by a copier looking through files. "This is Julie Klam."

We looked at each other hard. He was not dorky with glasses and a bad haircut. He was very handsome and bald and wearing an untucked pocket T.

"How did things go with Tom Cruise?" he asked.

"Oh, fine. He tried to steal my *Pop-Up* script. He wants to make a new movie called *Funny Things I've Noticed About the Wallflowers' 'One Headlight' Video.*"

Paul did a mock Yosemite-Sam-smoke-coming-out-the-ears expression. He was warm and friendly and I noticed he wasn't wearing a wedding band. I was grinning when I came out and took Joe downstairs.

"You're gonna be havin' lunches with that guy, right?" he said, jealous and angry.

"I hope so."

"Fuckin' credit-card guys," Joe spewed out the window.

A week later I was called in for an interview with Paul and the show's executive producers, Tad and Woody. I went into the Duane Reade downstairs to check my makeup and then went up. It was an interview unlike any other. Lots of funny questions and laughing and at the end I had to take a pop quiz: I had to name the celebrities pictured on the office's Wall of Fame.

"And . . . *go!*"

"Alan Alda, Doug Henning, Charlene Tilton, George Takei, Milton Berle, Catherine Bach, Timothy Hutton, Keith Moon." I had my back (and ass) to them the whole time.

"One hundred percent. First time ever."

Woody told me they were interviewing several other people and would be in touch. As I shook his hand, I said, "I hope they all suck."

I left feeling pretty good. Tad and Woody definitely liked me, though Paul looked miserable. I thought perhaps he was irritated by me. My attempts to be charming could have bugged him. Whatever. They had many other applicants who probably were far more suitable than I. I'd go home and forget it.

The following Friday I came in with Otto around five p.m. There was a message on my machine.

"Hi, Julie, this is Paul from *Pop-Up Video,* with Tad and Woody, and we wanted to tell you [different person's voice] YOU GOT THE JOB! BEATING OUT THOUSANDS

OF APPLICANTS! YOU, JULIE KLAM, ARE THE WINNER!! [Paul's somber voice:] Please call me at the office so I can give you the start-date info."

I listened to the message over and over, then called Paul back.

"Hey, congratulations!" He was friendly again. He gave me the whole story of what was expected of me and when to report. He also told me the salary was $1,000 a week. I told him that was up $1,000 a week from my current salary. I called my parents and played them the message. They couldn't understand what was being said but were really happy for me. My dad said, "I knew you could do it, kid." Though if I'd called my father and said I got a job as a studio head of Paramount or president of the United States or even chief of brain surgery at Mount Sinai he would have said the same thing. And then he'd talk about the early signs of my eventual success, like how well I drove in Manhattan and how David Letterman was crazy about me. These things, in his eyes, added up to major success in the field of my choice—politics, entertainment, or demigoditude.

Seconds after I accepted the position, panic set in. I was going to have to work. What were the hours? Was this one of those places where people worked through lunch? Would they let me leave early on Thursday nights to go to therapy? What if I got sick? What if I couldn't do it?

A normal person would have either had the thoughts and dealt with them or not had the thoughts. Not me. I decided to document my crazies and send my new boss an e-mail to let him know exactly who it was he had hired.

Thursday, April 1, 1999, 5:00 p.m.

Dear Mr. Leo,

I am so excited to start my new job as "writer" on *Pop-Up Video.* Having this assignment is already working as a real "guy magnet." I say, "Do you want to have sex? I work at *Pop-Up Video*?" And they almost always say, "Sure!"

I just wanted to ax you some questions, however, regarding protocol. But seriously, I am trying to get my non-working life squashed into the parameters of my new job life (dog walks, going to the gym, shrink appointments) and I wondered if you can tell me are there set hours or is this a stay-in-your-seat-till-the-job's-done job (which is fine, I don't shy away from hard work).

Also, is there a bathroom or is that something you feel we can handle "off hours"?

And, finally, if the need arises, can I bring an old Italian man to work?

I am anxiously awaiting April 5, 9:30 a.m., when I shall ring the bell on the bubble tank and enter my destiny.

Tanks,

Julie R. Klam

I had learned precious little since my *Interview* interview. I guess I had hid my ambivalence better this time—well enough to get hired, anyway. But once that happened, I couldn't stop myself from letting out how insecure and totally unfit I was to actually work there. I half expected him to write back, "Maybe this isn't the place for you." Instead I was surprised by his extremely kind and hilarious (and even flirtatious) response. And then I started to panic about how I'd come across—neurotic, lazy, slutty?

It turned out I had nothing to be afraid of. Paul made it easy for me. And even though we shared the secret of our e-mailing, he kept it totally professional. At the morning meeting he announced that there was a screening that night, at a bar uptown, of a show he had written and produced. It sounded mandatory, and by three o'clock I was panicking. It was the first day Otto was all alone. (I did have a dog walker come take him out for an hour, and I left a buffet of treats all over the apartment, the air-conditioning on, and classical music playing, but still he was bound to be missing me.) Thinking quickly, I told Paul that I had to leave right after work because the painters painting the outside of my building had accidentally broken my window. There were painters painting the outside of my building, but the rest of it was a total lie.

"Of course, you should go home," Paul said, looking concerned.

When I got home there was a message from him saying he hoped that it had all gone okay, and that if things were under control he really hoped I'd show up for the screening that night.

I called Jancee and played her the message.

"What do you think?" I asked. "Does that sound businesslike to you?"

"JESUS!" she yelled. "That is downright creepy. Don't go!"

Otto agreed with her. I fretted. I didn't want to miss my

first work function, and I did like Paul. Finally I decided to take Otto over to Mattie's and go to the thing. Everyone around me acted like I had gone mad. I finally had a good job and I did not appear to be taking care of it.

It ended up being a really fun night, and the *Pop-Up* special Paul had written and produced was brilliant. I was so proud to be a part of such a cool show. It had even been nominated for an Emmy.

The first day of work was a Monday, and by Wednesday I was draping myself across Paul's desk during script sessions. Subtlety, thy name ain't Julie. I really liked Paul, *really*. It was another example of the inability of my subconscious to stay out of my way. I'd been reading *Glamour* magazine since I was fifteen, so I knew that flirting with the boss was a no-no. Margot suggested waiting until after the season to explore the possibility of a relationship with him. As I piled up a take-out container at the *E. coli* salad bar during lunch, she and I talked on the phone. As always, she made several good points.

- If it was meant to be, it could wait.
- If we got together and it didn't work out, it would be very uncomfortable.
- If one of us was going to lose their job over an office romance, it wouldn't be Paul.

In my defense, I wasn't exactly working at Shearson Lehman. The production company, Spin the Bottle, had a fridge full of beer for the staff to partake of at any time of day. One of our bosses had a pierced chin and spent vacations experiencing the late-nineties drug culture at Burning Man Festival. It was a high-functioning office, to be sure, but there was a bit of bacchanalia thrown in.

So it was agreed. I would back off and start being professional. Margot also said I already had enough on my plate with the new job, and a new relationship might just tip the balance I didn't exactly have.

The work was challenging, but working with Paul was not. He made me laugh so much that I bit my lip so as not to appear loony. The way he made me feel was such a completely different experience than I had ever had before. He was the kind of guy I'd had crushes on my whole life, the guys with big personalities who made everyone laugh, but he was actually interested in me, too. Friday of my first week he asked me if I'd have dinner with him the following week. I agreed and went back and asked my officemate, Amy, if Paul had invited her to a dinner next week, which I assumed would include all the writers.

She shook her head and slowly said, "No." She had been trying to convince me that Paul *like*-liked me, and here was the final proof.

"Well, *I'm* going," I said. "Don't tell anyone!" I thought about what Margot had said, and weighed it against what I wanted to do. I felt like I was making an informed choice. Amy had a raging crush on the production manager, and we ended up sitting at our desks like two sappy teenagers who'd burst out laughing any time one of their pretend boyfriends walked by.

"I'm going out with him," I told my mother.

"Oh, good!" My mother, unlike Margot, felt that betting on my getting the guy was better than betting on my succeeding. It wasn't that she didn't believe in me—she was always remarking on how impressed she was by my talent—but in the end what felt safe to her was to be with an earner rather than trying to be an earner. It was fine if I *wanted* to make money; even my mother would make money sometimes, and it would go in an account for her to do fun things with. It was play money. My dad made the real money. I shouldn't *need* to make money. Because we just couldn't count on me to keep doing it.

The day of our first date Paul came by my desk and dropped off some script notes. He leaned down to me to show me something and whispered, "Meet me on the corner of Twenty-eighth and Sixth at seven o'clock. We can't walk out together."

That's when I realized it was real, and I got a huge stomachache. I wanted to go home.

I sent him another e-mail.

Dear Mr. Leo,

I'm concerned about this evening. Let's just please take it slow. But if it does happen to go well, I just want you to know I like emerald-cut diamonds—they sparkle more. Also, don't get it retail; you'll be marrying a Jewish girl, you know.

Sincerely,

Ms. Klam

This was my mother in me; she was a smart and excellent flirt. I'd never done this before and I was having fun. It didn't occur to me to worry about losing my job.

We met at the prescribed time and walked—with Paul's bike—to find a place to eat. The entire time I told him about how nervous I was that if this didn't work out, I'd be the one in trouble, et cetera.

"I'm not like that," he said. "I promise if it doesn't work out, it'll be fine. I won't fire you or anything."

"But will you assign me bad videos to pop?"

"Yes."

We had dinner and talked and talked and laughed and finally kissed. We kissed so much that several people on Sixth Avenue requested that we get a room.

I went and picked up Otto at Mattie's and told her that I was going to marry Paul. Mattie, always the romantic, said, "Get your dog outta here, I gotta go to bed."

I went home and lay awake all night thinking about Paul. I knew that he was the one. I felt it in my cells, like we had some past lives together. His name was Paul, my father's name. His birth date was November 10, 1964; my father's was November 11, 1934. We had both gone to high schools that were called John Jay (in different areas of New York State), and we both went to NYU, overlapping for two years. His brother had worked in the building that my insurance job was in at the same time. We could have met a million times. There was something else, too. He smelled right. No one that I had dated before had not offended my olfactory senses. Joe had taken so many showers that I had never even gotten to his smell. I read somewhere that people are attracted to people who have complementary DNA. That must have been it.

We decided to keep the relationship a secret at work, but after about a week I saw that wasn't a good idea. A group of writers converged in my office to talk about Paul, if his notes were fair, and if he drove us too hard. I realized that when our relationship eventually did come out, everyone was going to wonder what they had said to me in confidence that I might have betrayed, and that wouldn't be cool. At a staffers girl's night out I spilled it, and by the next morning there wasn't a soul at Spin the Bottle or VH1 who didn't know what was going on. There were a lot of mixed feelings that I wouldn't fully realize until later. Tad wanted to set up an office romance cam and turn it into a show for the website.

We started dating on April 14, and on May 22 I took him to Washington, D.C., to be my date at Matt's wedding to Lara, a psychologist who looked kind of like Matt might if he was put through a beautiful-woman machine. Though it seemed at the time like trial by fire, Paul was an instant hit among my family. Not only was he handsome, with a cool and well-paying job, but he was funny and kind. He entertained my parents at breakfast with an impression of Mr. Yuri, his Slavic barber, who was always trying to make Paul buy his son's used clothes, like a leather jacket with padded shoulders and a plethora of zippers. Mr. Yuri would snarl at him when he passed on the jacket. Perhaps more pressing to my family, Paul was also very obviously not a gangster. He didn't have an ex who was a crack whore with between three and six kids, depending on the day.

The following weekend was Memorial Day. We got together Friday night and stayed together until Monday night. Three days together with no breaks and at the end of it, when it was time for him to leave, I was utterly despondent.

Paul had told me weeks before, on our second date, that he loved me.

"No you don't," I said flatly.

"Yes I do."

"You can't love me, you don't know me."

"Well, I do. I love you."

I was irritated.

"I don't love you, yet."

"That's okay," he said.

When he left on Memorial Day, there was no uncertainty. I was intensely, recklessly, and passionately in love with Paul.

Six

Pu! Pu! Pu!
(Spit Three Times)

MY ENTIRE CHILDHOOD I used to do this thing. I'd get to a clean page in my diary and make a list of the things I needed to do to fix my life. It usually went something like: (1) Get better grades; (2) Lose weight; (3) Grow hair; (4) Grow nails. Sometimes my hair was long enough and my nails were fine. Lose weight and Get better grades, Get better grades and Lose weight. I had pretty much the same body-image issues as every other Young Miss in the country; I saw myself as morbidly obese even though I was perfectly normal. The grades, alas, did not need dysmorphia; they were truly awful. Midway through the second marking period of my tenth-grade year, I received five "interims" (the notice our school sent home to warn you that you were failing). I sat at the kitchen table opening one school envelope after another: Spanish, English, math, social studies, and biology.

"Oh, you poor thing!" my mother said. I wasn't grounded or anything. Over dinner, my family remarked on the sheer number of referrals.

"How many classes do you take, anyhow?" my dad asked, biting into an ear of corn.

"Seven," I said.

"Well, then, that's great!" my mother said with far too much enthusiasm. Because I hadn't received referrals in all of my classes. I didn't get one in gym because I was officially excused, and I didn't get one in music because the teacher, Gilbert Freeman, didn't "believe in that shit."

We ended up going to see an educational therapist, who tested me. Somehow I had missed acquiring the basic skills in almost everything. She marveled at it, asking if my parents had gotten divorced when I was in elementary school, or if someone had died.

"I was just out that day."

She said the best thing for me would be to leave tenth grade and go back to seventh to catch up. Fortunately, I was just allowed to fail quietly and not endure living a Rodney Dangerfield movie.

In college I got good grades but I gained a ton of weight. After college I lost weight but I didn't have a career. There was always something missing from the picture. Always at least one "needs improvement."

One June morning I was heading into work on the kind of day that is featured in hair-care commercials. It was a couple of months into my new job at *Pop-Up* and my new relationship with Paul, and I stopped and took stock. Everything Was Perfect. I felt slightly dizzy. It was the first time in my conscious life that I had felt that way. I loved my boyfriend, my job, my dog, even my hair. I stopped and looked ahead toward Times Square and thought, "Remember this time, for it may not last forever." (Whenever I talk to myself I use a very formal voice.)

When I started moving again, the feeling floated to the back of my mind and I felt slightly aware of the next thought: "What's going to happen to fuck this all up?" I was aware of the whole *kinehora* thing. When you're Jewish, acknowledging good luck invites the Evil Eye in to mess up your kid's vision, or dent your fender, or give you chronically weak nails, unless you follow it with *"Kinehora."*

Five months after we met, Paul and I started looking for a place together. We'd both outgrown our places and had wanted to move, and now we had a reason. Neither of our apartments was suitable for two people to live in. At mine you had to climb a ladder to go to sleep, and his place was just a dump. His rent was $324 a month—roughly one-third of the market rate—and if you asked me, he was being overcharged.

Though it was billed as a one-bedroom apartment, it was more of a single room with a bathtub in the middle of it. There was a small, unlit closet with a door that didn't shut all the way; this was where the toilet was. Paul had sweetly hung Christmas lights on the ceiling so that you felt vaguely celebratory every time you had to pee. For reading material, he had tacked up the rantings of various East Village maniacs that had been posted on utility poles around his neighborhood or left on cars.

There had been several attempts to paint the walls in a range of colors in the gray family. There was nowhere to sit, except on his ratty futon, which was balanced on a crate in a spot where the floor was so slanted you'd roll into the wall if you lay there. It was like a funhouse, except it wasn't fun, or a house. With the giant hole in the wall, you didn't have to wonder what the rodents were up to. You could see them in the wall. Even they had a nicer place than Paul. I had recently been to the Lower East Side Tenement Museum to see how new immigrants to the city lived in the last century. Same as Paul, but cleaner.

The only wall hanging was a cardboard "cameo" of Abraham Lincoln, the kind they hang in a classroom around Presidents' Day. It broke my heart because it was done without irony; Paul loved Abraham Lincoln. He'd look at the picture and talk about Lincoln's life, the Civil War, the Emancipation Proclamation: "His achievements were of biblical proportions." I thought Lincoln would look good next to my framed portrait of Lou Gehrig.

Neither of us had a clue about rents. We thought since we currently paid under $400 a month each, a thousand a month would be enough to get us a classic six on Central Park West. Then we started looking. Our first open house was advertised in *The New York Times* as a garden duplex in a West Eighties brownstone for $1,100 a month. We feverishly readied our paperwork and started discussing the vegetables we would plant. By the time we arrived a line snaked around the block, but it moved quickly. You could smell the mold from the hall. It was a dark, cramped shithole and the tomatoes would've had a hard time in the paved yard. It was a garden duplex in the same way that a pothole in the rain is a natural lake. Very quickly we raised our target figure to $1,500 a month, and then to $2,000. We saw a lot of boxy, ugly new apartments that we both hated, even with their "free health club" (actually, one stationary bicycle from 1970). There was also the issue of the dog, my dog, Otto. Paul had not been a dog person when we met—he let me know that. I was very much a dog person, the kind who talked to other dog people about what colors looked best on my Otto (red and royal blue—he was black and white, a "winter"). He was my boy, I loved him, and, transference be damned, I did not want him to feel abandoned or displaced by my new relationship. My worst fights with Paul were over my putting Otto before him, either going straight home after work so he wouldn't be alone any longer than he needed to or sneaking Otto into Paul's bed after he asked me not to (the floor was cold and dusty and Otto didn't like it). I never pushed their relationship, which is why they ultimately became best mates. A startling and gifted artist, Paul did a study of Otto in charcoal no different from the Mona Lisa, if the sitter were a walleyed, pancake-faced dog with a runny nose. But I digress. . . . There were many apartments that just simply didn't accept dogs, no matter how photogenic they were.

When the broker, who got fifteen percent of the annual

rent, brought us into the building on Riverside Drive, a dog-friendly prewar doorman building with stained-glass windows depicting grapevines in the lobby, we nearly wept. The apartment had been recently vacated by a dead woman who had lived there for fifty years. She was Italian and Jewish; Paul is Italian and I am Jewish, so it seemed serendipitous. Livia Morpugo and her brother, Dante, Holocaust survivors, lived in the one-bedroom together. He had died four years earlier, and when she passed away there were no Morpugos left, so her stuff sat there, orphaned. Among the ruins were her "icebox," a 1947 Bakelite Philco radio, and yellowed newspaper clippings taped to the doors—ads for exotic travels around the world for under $400. A phone had never been installed.

By the time we moved in, the renovations that allowed our landlord to charge us six times Livia's rent of $375 a month had eradicated every trace of her. Clean, white tiles concealed the formerly gray immigrant bathroom and kitchen walls. Paul and I bought our own Ralph Lauren paint in three colors—Beach Cabana, Pavilion, and Sailboat—for the landlord's painters to use, rather than their offer of free two-tone beige/darker beige, which, we were told, "people go for."

We had loads of asinine anxiety fights before the big moving day. My sentimental favorite happened a week before we were to move. Paul started arguing with me about how he always had to come to my apartment and I never came to his. I reminded him that in six days his apartment and my apartment would be one and the same.

"I'm just saying!" he fumed.

We moved in on December 1 and started filling our new home. Paul brought nothing from his apartment. There, in place of furniture, he had intentions. I had a few things, but most of them Paul hated, so we started from scratch and spent fortunes on Moroccan chests, antique Chinese bureaus, Persian hooked rugs. A decorator could not have done better, and we were very happy with our new home. Many times when I felt on the verge of leaving, I thought, "What about the furniture?" You have to give a relationship a little more effort when there are fine furnishings involved. Recalling King Solomon, I thought about slicing the Tibetan cabinet in two. No, that would not do.

We were being enveloped by our ABC Carpet & Home sofa when my mother called.

"Daddy and I decided this year for Hanukkah to take the whole family—spouses, kids, and significant others—on an all-expense-paid trip to Barbados," she said like a game-show announcer. "We're renting a house on the beach with a cook and a housekeeper, so we'll have a choice of eating at home or going to one of the nearby elegant cafés."

It was very amusing that she included my father in the "decided." My father had a long history of hating beach vacations. In all of our photos, Brian, Matthew, my mother, and I romp about the waves or lie browning in the sand, while way in the background, barely visible under a lone tree, my father sits glowering, under a Woody Allen hat, with white Hilton towels around his shoulders and on his legs.

Paul was impressed; he said it felt like a Kennedy-clan

thing. I was excited about the trip, but I also felt like it was a down payment on my dowry. Like my grandparents furnishing my mother and father's first home, my parents were giving Paul a gift that he would not be getting if he wasn't with me, and the idea was to send the message "Stick around, there's more where that came from."

Originally, Matt and his new wife, Lara, and Brian and his wife, Cheryl, and their baby, Sadie, were all going to come.

First Matt bailed. I e-mailed him and begged him to reconsider. He wrote back:

> I think we are too old to be going on a family vacation together, and there won't be enough to do, no place to get lost, on a beach. I don't know. Too many personalities. Personally, I like to go places alone. Otherwise, I'm always worried about what people will think of my pimples. I also think the harmony we felt growing up, sitting in front of the fire, lying on dogs, requires dogs, and that here in our thirties we will be forced to lie on each other, with only Father being furry enough to be a dog.

Then Cheryl, whom I hesitate to call an in-law because she is a sister to me and a wonderful presence in our family gatherings, also bowed out. On the previous family trip to Bermuda, Matt and I were solo but it was Cheryl I spent time with, lunching, drinking spritzers, lying on the beach (even though she wore a gigantic hat that shielded people on other islands from the sun). No one was more disappointed than me, except her. She was pregnant and had gone into preterm labor at twenty-one weeks. Even though they stopped it and it looked like she was stabilized, the trip would be in her twenty-fourth week and her doctor said she probably didn't want to deliver a preemie in Barbados. At first Brian was going to stay home, too, but then he thought it would be good for Cheryl to have Sadie, who at nineteen months didn't understand why Mommy couldn't get out of bed, away from there. So it would just be Paul and me, my parents, and Brian and Sadie. Less and less of a party crowd by the second.

But the biggest spoiler ended up being me. Two days before we were due to leave, and two weeks after my period was late, I discovered that I, too, was pregnant. I felt like I had been shot; the honeymoon was over before we got on the plane.

I was absolutely certain that I wasn't ready to be a mother. How could I be if I had been irresponsible enough to get knocked up? Paul felt the same way, though he was more focused on the fact that when the test came out positive, the first people I wanted to tell were my mother and Mattie. Then him. It was a knee-jerk reaction. Paul thought it was a very bad sign that I looked to my mother and aunt for comfort and only when I was all taken care of would I let him in on it.

"So what did they say?" Paul said, covering his anger.

"My mom said, 'Oops,'" I reported. "And Mattie said she thought brides with pregnant bellies were cute."

There was no way in hell I was going to be a pregnant bride. I had a very specific vision of that day, and it didn't include a Vera Wang maternity dress and bloated arms.

I called my OB, who said it was too early for a D&C; I would have to wait till I got back from Barbados. It just kept getting better. At least I wasn't thinking about the *kinehora* thing anymore.

The irony of the most beautiful island being the setting for our hell wasn't lost on us. Being pregnant and waiting to terminate. Starving and exhausted, eating like crazy and being superemotional. Wearing a sexy bathing suit with my breasts feeling all weird. Paul and I were suddenly very unsure of each other. And then throw in Sadie's crying day and night, which we later found out was a double ear infection, though Brian told me that he had arranged it so I wouldn't feel bad about not having a baby.

But I did. No matter how I convinced myself I was, I wasn't. So we all felt cruddy. I was a shark with one purpose and no peripheral vision. Put the blinders on and get it done, which was why it was so painful that I had to wait. I didn't want time to think. I spent most of the day walking up and down the beach, picking up sea glass. I amassed an enormous collection of pale green, lapis blue, soft, clear, and rubbed smooth as velvet by the sea. Paul started helping me, and it became our focus. Find good sea glass. Focus on sea glass.

Paul described me as "miserable and mute." I felt like my mouth was glued shut. I thought we should break up, but we had signed a two-year lease. I had to think about the furniture.

Staring out at the Caribbean Sea, that unbearably stunning turquoise, aquamarine, azure, my favorite sight in the world, made me want to heave. I felt like a grotesque monster in one of my mother's Mrs. Roper muumuus. At least the beach was empty and there was no one to compare myself to. And then two little specks appeared on the horizon; they were swimming toward us, getting clearer. Soon they weren't specks, they were people. And not just people, but a stunning model with flowing blond locks and wearing a silver string bikini, and her beau, with skin like my Bottega Veneta bag and his luggage in an economic Speedo. We watched them drop their scuba equipment and plop down in the sand to watch the sea.

"That's Rod Stewart," I told Paul. They say your senses are heightened during pregnancy; my strongest sense was celebrity spotting. I didn't even have my glasses on.

Paul smiled for the first time. "You're hallucinating rock-star mirages."

"Look." I was fully prepared to defend my observation. "She is a model, for sure. He is older, and European, based on the Speedo and his blatant disregard for sunblock. And, finally, your honor, that chicken-style hairdo sticking up." I felt a little better.

We continued to observe them.

"Do you really think it's him?" Paul said, squinting.

"No, I know it's him."

The model rose up and sauntered toward our beach house, not an ounce of fat on her impossibly long tanned legs. I wanted Paul to bury me in the sand. Everything but my nostrils.

"What the hell?" Paul said when the guy turned in profile. "We popped him," he chirped. "'Do Ya Think I'm Sexy,'

'Forever Young,' 'Downtown Train'"—he was counting on his hands—"and what's the one in black-and-white with his—what was her name?—and she's hanging around a pool and he's watching her from a hotel room through binoculars or something?"

"'Infatuation,'" I said.

"We also did a live version of a 'Hot Legs' duet between him and Tina Turner," he recalled.

I nodded.

"I'm going over there," Paul said, not moving. It was odd: we lived in New York, where we wouldn't dream of approaching a celebrity, but here it was different. I didn't want to, but I was curious to see Paul's attempt.

I watched as Rod listened to Paul and then nodded vigorously and laughed and Paul talked and Rod talked and Rod pointed to the ocean and Paul pointed to the house. They stood up together, Paul scooped up the scuba gear, and they headed back toward me.

"Rod needs to go through our house to get to the street," Paul said intensely. "There's this catamaran of paparazzi out there following them."

"Of course!" I said, and jumped up to escort them. Both Paul and I got very into the crisis, as if the paparazzi boat were armed rebels. When we got to the front of the house, Miss Model was walking around, looking for an escape route.

"They're taking us through their house," Rod said in Rod Stewart's voice. Model followed. I didn't enjoy looking at her up close; no one ever needs to see a stomach that flat. I wondered if she'd had some organs removed.

We entered the bungalow, and my parents and Brian and the cook were all hunched over the sink, consumed by something. As we were charging by I said, "Mom, is it okay if Rod Stewart walks through our house?" to get them to look up. They did.

"We'll be back for dinner!" Rod said as he and the model slipped out the front door. We all cracked up, desperately needing something to laugh at.

Later my mother commented that he was "nice-looking but no Rudolph Valentino." I remember feeling that fierce irritation only a daughter can feel for her mother. For my whole life, my mom talked about who didn't measure up to Rudolph Valentino. Rick Savage on the varsity football team, or the guy our neighbor was having an affair with.

"Mom, no one has considered Rudolph Valentino as being the pinnacle of handsomeness for a hundred years!"

"Sorry," she said sarcastically, correcting to, "He's no *Robert Redford*."

"Robert Redford is almost seventy!"

"What do you want me to say?"

The whole group looked at me like I was a hormonal nutbag.

"Leonardo DiCaprio?" I suggested.

"Ucch, Julie, he's twelve years old!" she snapped. "That's disgusting."

And thus ended the highlight of the trip.

Seven

Outlook Not So Good

WE GOT HOME on Sunday, and on Tuesday I had the procedure. Paul was there; though it wasn't easy, I kept my mother and Mattie away.

"But we always go to each other's abortions!" Mattie joked.

"It's what we do!" my mother added.

"Ma, Paul's paying for it, he should go if he wants," I said, sounding more and more like she did when she talked to her mother.

It was terrible, but Paul was wonderful. He came into the room where I was recovering and without saying a word put my socks on. He knew my feet were always cold. I remember wondering in a Valium haze why doctors make you take your socks off. It's so much better to have them on.

Concurrently, something had begun to happen with Paul. He was drinking a tremendous amount of juice and peeing constantly. And he lost about thirty-five pounds in six weeks. I was alarmed and told him to go to the doctor. He didn't have anyone he liked, so I called Dr. Pegler, my beloved pediatrician, whom I was still going to. (No one wanted to leave her. First the rule was when you got married you had to go; then she changed it to when you had a baby.) She recommended a terrific GP and Paul made an appointment for Friday, still several days away. It was a long week.

The day of his appointment, Paul didn't go to work. He just wasn't feeling well. It turned out that neither was I; I went in and left because I was throwing up. When he got out of bed to go to the doctor, I got in. His appointment was at one p.m. I lay in bed waiting for him to come home and take care of me. I began watching the front door—2:30, 3:00, 3:30, 4:00, 4:15, 4:20, 4:21. I had a terrible feeling I would not see Paul walk back in the door before I walked out of it. He didn't have a cell phone, and I was getting up to look up the doctor's number when the phone rang. The caller ID read "Lenox Hill Hospital."

"Paul?"

"Hi."

"Where are you?"

"I'm in the emergency room. It's diabetes."

"What?" I was nearly hyperventilating. I recalled a scene

when I was twelve, sitting at the kitchen table, and Brian burst in the kitchen door, terror-stricken.

"Jeff Dugan got hit by a car!"

My mother, who was cooking dinner, said, *"What?"*

And I thought, "Why is she saying 'What?'" She heard him, and it's wasting time! And there I was, saying, "What?"

"I have diabetes. My blood sugar is very high."

"Okay. What are they doing?"

"Trying to give me insulin to lower the level. If they can't, they're going to admit me."

"So when are you coming home?"

"Probably not today."

I was still throwing up, but I jumped in a cab and headed for Lenox Hill. I didn't throw up in the cab. I did throw up in the hospital. They told me I couldn't stay. I was sort of puzzled that I was being thrown out of a hospital for being sick. I did see Paul briefly, and he looked terrible: pale and clammy, with storm clouds under his eyes.

I don't know about emergency rooms in Vermont or North Beverly Hills, but I've been in more than my share of Manhattan ERs, and they aren't happy places. It's usually me and the person I'm with and a large number of screaming people and homeless people and walls the color of vomit, or a bruise, or mucus. I know, I know, it's an emergency room, not the Four Seasons, but it still strikes me as odd. Not the decor, but the clientele. Why don't you ever see anyone from the society pages—Blaine Trump or Oscar de la Renta or chic celebrities like Gwyneth Paltrow or

Robert De Niro? You just don't, though I have seen no fewer than three people in the ER with HATE tattooed on their knuckles. It's sort of like jury duty in that way. Not particularly good for people-watching.

"I'm so sorry," I said, retching out the door.

By some stroke of luck, Matt was in New York from D.C., and he came over to bring me saltines and walk Otto.

I felt very weak and scared and I wanted Matt to stay a while.

I recalled the time I was sick when I was eight and Matt was ten. I had been sleeping in bed with the flu, and when I woke up Matt was walking by my room. I asked him if he could please ask Mom to make me cream cheese on raisin toast. He brought it up a few minutes later. I asked for another one. He brought that, too. Then I asked if Mom was coming up soon.

"She's not home," he said.

I couldn't believe it. Matt had made the cream cheese on raisin toast for me.

"Thank you, Matthew."

"Sure," he said.

He took care of me a lot. Sometimes I thought it was why he didn't want to live near me. He felt responsible for me and it was too great a burden. Mattie frequently told the story of when she came to baby-sit us for a weekend. I was crying in my crib, so I was probably one or a little older. So Matt was around three. He came in to where she was sleeping, woke her up, and said, "Please take care of my baby sister."

. . .

After Matt left, I lay in bed, trying to talk myself into feeling better: Tomorrow it will all be okay. I will ask Paul where fancy rich people go when they accidentally drive a nail into their toe or bleed internally. Then we can make jokes and pretend that everything is normal.

The phone rang at seven the next morning. It was Paul asking for some books. I told him I'd be there right after I showered and got dressed and walked Otto. He said he was feeling the same, bored, and he didn't like the hospital.

"How about you?" he asked.

"All better, thanks," I said. Never in my life had those words been uttered by me. The best I could ever admit was "As well as can be expected . . . under the circumstances." All better, thanks. It was like I had become English or Catholic overnight.

I dressed carefully, and as I slipped my sweater on, Grandma Pearl's tiny head popped up on my shoulder, her hair sprayed into a red-brick nautilus shell: *"Show them you're rich and fancy, you'll be treated better."*

Whenever we went back to visit our old friends in White Plains, Grandma Pearl told me to wear my jewelry. I was seven and the only thing I had was an enamel Raggedy Ann necklace with moving arms and legs. It was my childhood bling. I wore it like it was a bulletproof vest.

According to my grandmother, there were two reasons why Jews wore/owned a lot of diamonds:

1. God forbid there was another Hitler, our fortunes would be portable and easily carried into exile.
2. When your kids get in trouble in school, you have to load on a lot of diamonds to intimidate the teacher. The worse the infraction, the heavier the jewelry. (Though when we kids were in school, my grandmother would ask us how things were going, and if we didn't like a teacher, she offered to buy the school and fire the person.)

Grandma's regular, everyday jewelry was her engagement ring, a 7.5-carat pear-shaped stone with side diamonds, and her wedding band, thirteen half-carat to one-carat marquise diamonds. Piling it on was a blinding affair. There were pins, bracelets, earrings, necklaces. You needed cataract sunglasses to look at her.

There was a time when I never wanted any article of clothing that didn't have the brand emblazoned on it. I had a Diane von Furstenberg velour shirt with a big DVF, Gloria Vanderbilt jeans, and a sweatshirt that screamed SASSOON! with the A-okay symbol. Then I began to notice that the elite Bedford preppies never wore logos, just my Jewish brethren, burdened by fields of polo players. I reasoned that if you came over on the *Mayflower*, there was no need to tell people you'd arrived. Look at any history book; those

Pilgrims had buckles everywhere—on their shoes, jackets, hats—but none of them, not a single one, said PRADA.

I WALKED INTO Paul's hospital room, and my warm-up comedy patter quickly morphed into barely breathing. The room was jammed with white coats. Holding court was a doctor who resembled an elderly Cary Grant. An entire class of residents hung on his every word, taking copious notes. In the middle of the pack lay the lab specimen, Paul.

Their heads whiplashed over to me when the door squeaked open. They all stared at me, I guess looking for some sign of breeding or standing in the community. Nothing sparkled on my hand or ears; I briefly considered doing a cartwheel so at least the label of my TSE cashmere sweater would be visible. All those doctors! My grandmother was shaking her chains from the grave: "Forget the guy in the bed, go for the one with the stethoscope and the hair plugs!"

"Is this your wife?" Dr. Cary Grant asked Paul.

"My girlfriend," Paul answered weakly.

"You should marry her," he said.

They went back to ignoring me and I stood in a corner of the room. The doctor outlined the things Paul should eat and the exercise he needed to do, and said that a nurse would visit with him to show him how to give himself insulin injections. He mentioned to the students that Paul's blood sugar was so high when he was admitted that another day or so and he would've gone into a diabetic coma.

Paul looked at me through the circle of white jackets. I

squeezed through the line and held his hand. He clutched me awkwardly and I didn't move.

I was at the hospital from early morning until visiting hours ended, and with the exception of a visit from Paul's oldest brother and his wife and son, it was just me. I was struck that Paul's mother didn't come to visit. After all, I was his girlfriend of less than a year, and she was his mother. She called to say she had a financial appointment that she couldn't reschedule. I wondered why it didn't seem strange to Paul.

Five days later, I took Paul home in a cab. Life, as we had barely known it, would never be the same. Paul had to eat different foods, no sugar, low carbs—and this was the man who used to get a brownie the size of my head to go with his afternoon coffee. No alcohol because of the interactions with the drugs, and no grapefruit, for the same reason. It was mind-numbing. He needed to incorporate regular exercise, along with frequently checking his blood sugar with a glucose monitor that required pricking his finger, and taking insulin, which meant injecting himself with a needle. It was horrible and depressing for both of us. Every time I left our apartment, I had the urge to run and keep on going, but I did the opposite.

My caretaking skills kicked in and I became Florence Nightingale. The first day Paul was home I left with a list:

Go to Duane Reade and drop off seven prescriptions.
Buy a WaterPik (diabetics have dental problems).
Get special socks (diabetics have foot problems).
Buy the glucose monitor.

Make a long list of diabetic-friendly groceries, and buy them.

Go back to Duane Reade and pick up the prescriptions.

After the last item was checked on my list, I took off for home. The bags were so heavy that I stopped walking every couple of steps and rested, and I am no weakling. And more than strength, I have an unwavering will. At one point, a block away from the apartment, I considered getting a cab. Then Paul called on my cell phone and asked me to please hurry; he needed his insulin. I ran.

Exhausted from the hospital stay and the stress, Paul mostly slept. I tried making foods from a diabetic cookbook I bought. I wanted to eat with him, make like it was nothing, but it was grim. Paul and I shared a love of planning dinner at ten in the morning (well, maybe that was just me). How do you adjust to this? We had a pregnancy, an abortion, and diabetes, all in less than a two-week period. I was ill-equipped for any sort of crisis and here I was with back-to-back stomach punches.

Both of us were the youngest in our families. Oftentimes I had this vision of us as two babies in a hospital nursery, wahh-wahhing because our diapers needed changing. Though Paul had always taken care of himself, working his way through high school and college, taking a job at the farmer's market to subsidize his first job in the MTV library, hitchhiking cross-country to work on a salmon boat in Alaska, I had not. When adversity hit in my life, a team of specialists led by my mother swooped in to save the day.

In fact, Jancee and I had a lifelong deal that we would make each other's unpleasant phone calls, since our voices, as well as our manner of speech, were the same. One editor I met with was so freaked out he had trouble interviewing me for a job because he said my "timbre was identical to Jancee's."

Though my support system could've beaten the crap out of Dr. Phil, they weren't really welcome here. Paul wanted us to depend on each other, and I was willing to give it a go, for him. This was "our" problem. It was a whole new way of dealing.

I looked forward to going to work, sitting in my cube with my headphones on, watching the same video over and over and over, Nirvana's "Smells Like Teen Spirit," and before I knew it, I wouldn't be thinking of diabetes or babies or weddings or diamonds, just the pains in Kurt Cobain's stomach that ultimately sent him over the brink to suicide.

Margot and I had been down to a phone session once a week, or once every other week, when I could make it, but after everything that had happened, I needed more. I went to therapy in the mornings before work when I wasn't going to the gym, and during the day I'd sneak out to the fire escape and call her. I couldn't afford to miss work, and I couldn't afford to miss therapy. With Paul's crisis, he needed all of his energy to focus on himself. Our talk of the future halted, and I wondered what was going to happen.

"Just take it one step at a time," Margot said. "You've been through a lot. The abortion, Paul's hospitalization. This is new for you."

Amen to that. Margot and I talked a lot about how unprepared I was for work, but now we had a new topic: how unprepared I was for *everything*. Whatever the stresses I had growing up, they didn't involve anyone close to me getting sick or dying. I knew kids in school whose parents died, but mine didn't even get colds. It wasn't till tenth grade that my one grandmother died, and the event was very distant for me. She was far away in a hospital in Florida, and I was in a high school production of Sean O'Casey's *Juno and the Paycock*. There was no funeral for her, just a vague promise from a mortician that her ashes would be scattered over the ocean by his friend, a deep-sea fisherman.

Jancee and I were sitting at the lunch counter at Bergdorf's eating lobster salad sandwiches when I told her what was going on.

"Oh, Jul," she said sympathetically. "Is there anything I can do?"

"You're doing it."

Despite her grueling schedule at *Rolling Stone*, working as a vee-jay on MTV2, and being interviewed for every entertainment show on the planet regarding her recent explosive breaking of *the* major entertainment story of the year, the identity of the father of Melissa Etheridge's children (David Crosby), she was there for me.

In my list of complaints, I mentioned that since I'd gotten my period, I'd been bleeding for thirty-eight days.

"That's not normal," she said, taking her cell phone out and dialing my doctor for me.

The nurse said I should've called earlier (I apologized)

and told me to make an appointment for a sonogram at a women's imaging center near my apartment.

"Can we please look at shoes?" I said, handing the phone back to Jancee.

On the way, we tucked into the cool clothes section. There were a bunch of hair bands on display, and Jancee put one on to make me laugh. She looked like she was going to wash her face. She's (not always intentionally) very funny trying things on. You can tell a lot about people by the expression they make when they're sampling sunglasses. Most people do the Angelina Jolie / supermodel cheek suck. Jancee, well, she does this big toothy grin that makes her look like a kid at summer camp who has just won a medal and has yet to find out that everyone else is getting a prize, too.

Approaching the shoe sale, I became aware that it wasn't going to work today. Staring wistfully at the racks of left-foot shoes—Christian Louboutin, Jimmy Choo, Manolo Blahnik—I was transported back to a time when my worst stress was outrunning a fellow linebacker to the size 10½ Ann Demeulemeester boots. I left without even donning one socklet.

At the office I received a package from Leslie, my good friend from high school. It contained pink-and-purple flip-flops and fun ponytail holders with sequined flowers on them. A cheer-up-you-had-an-abortion-and-your-boyfriend-has-diabetes gift.

Despite the outpouring of aid, I felt sickeningly alone. I went in for the sonogram, and sure enough, there was a wad of tissue left inside me. I think they should use a different word for a sonogram when a baby isn't involved. Call it a looksee-otomy.

"That's a bummer," the nurse said compassionately. She had a nose ring and fuschia hair. "You're going to have to get another one."

"Another what?" I said.

She wrinkled her face. "D&C."

"Motherfuckin' fuck." I said, which I wouldn't have said if she'd been the dignified Irish nurse I'd spoken to earlier.

"I agree," she said. "Fucks all around."

"A whole D&C? Can't they just Dustbust it?"

"Right," she said, sharing my sense of injustice.

I went back to the OB, this time skipping the Valium and taking the number 2 train back to work afterward.

I am the least likely person in the world to suffer silently. If I have a bruise on my leg I outline it in red pen, with several arrows pointing at it, so I get the attention I crave. But Paul had stolen my thunder with his life-threatening disease. In illness poker, diabetes trumps an abortion. We weren't just dealing with Paul's condition, either; his family history was equally awful. His father had died of heart disease and diabetes at age forty-two, leaving his mother with four sons to raise. Paul's father's father had died young, too, for the same reasons. One of the secrets Paul shared with me in that hospital room was that he never thought he'd live to see age forty. He was thirty-five.

For my part, I was just making it up as I went along. I was so worried about Paul. I needed a little help and Margot gave me the name of a therapist for Paul to see. He went easily.

A couple of months later, we were breathing a little better. Paul's blood-sugar levels were down. He was responding well to the plethora of medications, even getting low blood sugar at times. Normal didn't mean what it used to, but we were feeling it. And then I started to get antsy. I had been with Paul through some serious shit and we still felt the same way about each other, in love and sticking with it. The road ahead of us had disappeared in heavy fog, but I was willing to stay on it, and for that I felt I should be rewarded . . . with a diamond engagement ring.

There is a certain kind of person—a spelunker, or Ram Dass—who doesn't mind not knowing what comes next. A person who is not me. Everything in our world was a big question mark, but we knew we wanted to be together. So why couldn't we just set a date? Because one of us wasn't ready, and it wasn't me.

So just nine months into the relationship, we began the tug of war. Some days I'd sit at my desk and send Paul e-mails that said, "Are you ready now? How about now? Now? How about now? Are you ready now?" And he'd write back, "No, no, no, ye— no."

Margot and I decided that this would be a good time to lay off Paul and focus on enjoying myself. It had been a while since I had. I needed to throw myself into something other than worrying about my boyfriend's health and trying to get engaged.

As a kid, I was always jealous of my brother's hobbies. When Matt started collecting coins, Brian began assembling paper money.

"What can I collect?" I whined to my mother.

"Oh, let's see," she said and gave it some thought. "What are you interested in?"

Duh. If I had been interested in anything I wouldn't be asking. It was another one of those "the boys do this, the girls do that." In truth I had a dollhouse that my mother had made me herself, cutting the wood, gluing the wallpaper, laying the carpet, and furnishing it. That was something I had as a hobby, but I didn't realize it. So I decided to anoint myself with the goo of stamps—I would be a philatelist. As with everything, I was much more captivated by the notion of doing it than actually doing it. My father's father, Grandpa Willie, was the only one who really got into it. The weekend after I made my announcement, he delivered to me a large loose-leaf binder that in gold print announced itself as a STAMP COLLECTER'S BOOK. Preprinted pages had places for the various stamps I would be collecting. However, the only stamps I could get my hands on were the ones that came on the letters that were sent to us, the ordinary ten-centers, the ones we had in rolls of a hundred. Needless to say, there was no place in the book for the only stamp I had. Very quickly the hobby was laid to rest, at least as far as everyone but Grandpa Willie was concerned. For years I received envelopes that when opened revealed a ripped corner of an envelope featuring a stamp from England or Spain fastened with a paper clip. I received these missives till he died, the last one a beauty from Trinidad, where his nursing-home aide was from.

Though I was burned by stamp collecting, it did teach me

something: Don't start a collection until you have at least one of something, and try not to collect something you could not care less about.

During my NYU years, when I was particularly taken with Peter Bogdanovich's film *Paper Moon*, I was at the big flea market on Sixth Avenue and Twenty-fifth Street. While waiting for Barbara to try on some smelly vintage dress, I began going through a box of real photo postcards, pictures that were taken in photo studios at the turn of the century with props and backdrops. There was one of a World War I soldier in uniform saluting before an American flag; another of a bunch of people in old-fashioned bathing costumes posing in the midst of hand-painted waves, complete with mermaids and fierce sea monsters; and another of a bunch of guys in an "aeroplane." The last photo in the box was in terrible condition. It was badly creased, one edge ripped, but the image stopped my heart. A lovely couple, nervously posing on a wonderful paper moon, like the one Tatum O'Neal sat in. I had to have it and started figuring out how much I had on me, if I should run to the Citibank. Coolly, I requested a price.

"Oh my God," the man said, rolling his eyes, "take it, it's a mess."

I thanked him and fled before he realized the error of his ways. I kept the photo in the corner of my vanity mirror, never failing to be captivated by it. The romance of the moon, the tiny stars, the soft clouds, the expressions of the couple, their great costumes—her long skirt and high-necked blouse, ostrich-feather hat, and his elegant suit, which of course were their regular clothes. I looked in every flea market, asked everyone dealing in ephemera, and I never saw another one.

Then along came the Internet. With the new easy access to the world of dealers and auctions, I quickly amassed over a hundred and fifty paper moons. At night I sat on my bed and laid them out, separating them into categories: children, couples, women, men, single women, single men, dogs. When a particularly amazing one came up for auction, I developed complicated strategies. Sometimes I won, as with the prize moon I have with four people in Halloween costumes, and sometimes I didn't, as with the Santa Claus–like gentleman holding a screaming baby.

I questioned the dealers about the history. I'd always thought the song "It's Only a Paper Moon" inspired the backdrops, but it was written in 1933, after the postcards had long faded. At the time they were popular, though, the hit songs included "Shine On, Harvest Moon" and "By the Light of the Silvery Moon" and another one simply called "Moonbeams," so the delightful, puckish man in the moon was certainly in the zeitgeist.

My friend Bruce, a dealer in Pennsylvania, had given it a lot of thought, too. "The moon was always a mystery to man, but my gut theory is very simple. It's all about love . . . spooning under a moon, romance, mystery, wonderment." Bruce didn't talk, he spun yarns. "By the time the moon photo prop first turned up, everyone had either looked up to the sky and wondered . . . or had sat on a porch swing with their sweet thing, while the old folks inside pasted their ears to the window to make sure nobody got out of line." I liked that notion. I was a great romanticizer of moons and ye olde days. So that's what I focused on while I waited for Paul to lasso the moon.

Though he and I were working the same hours at the same place, I took over the running of the apartment—cleaning, cooking, and doing the laundry. Paul made money better than I did, but I kept our apartment better. I made a little money and Paul helped a little around the house. One night I asked Paul to put the wash in, and he came back upstairs with too many quarters.

"What happened?" I inquired.

"It all fit into one washer," he said proudly.

I walked Otto and called Jancee to "share." She'd lived with men before.

"I have a complaint," I said.

"Oh, good. What is it?" Jancee and I loved complaining to each other. She had actually stopped being friends with a woman, Cathy, when we met because she was always putting a happy face on every situation. Jancee and I preferred the pained face.

I told her about Paul's "help." "Nothing in the middle of the washer could oscillate!" I said.

"Oh please, they're all like that," she said, apologizing for chewing some weird health-food-store cookie she was into at the moment. "I call it 'toddler helping.' Because they make a big show of doing it and you have to give them tons of praise and then do it over when they walk out of the room. Just like a toddler. You know how you're baking something and a toddler drags a chair over and climbs onto it and you think, 'Oh no, oh please go watch a video.'"

"It's true!" I said. "And now I won't ask him to do it again."

She responded, "I'm sure he'll be real brokenhearted."

Otto squatted down and I stopped for him.

"That's their plan, you know," she continued. "Do it badly and then you won't ask again."

So laundry became my personal arena, though it gave me undue stress. I became possessed with amassing quarters. You'd think I'd just hit the lotto when one of my purchases came to something and twenty-five cents. And then I needed to strategize to get enough machines and worry about the people who left their stuff in the dryers that I needed. Other people had no problem taking strangers' laundry out of machines and plopping it on the table. When I did it, I'd call the elevator, whip the stuff out of the machine, throw mine in, and make a fast getaway. I was so scared of getting yelled at for touching someone else's stuff. Why didn't the management post some kind of protocol?

One night I went down around seven-thirty, when the room was usually deserted except for the big puddles of suds coming up through the grates on the floor. Three machines were in use and one was out of order, which left me two. Not enough. I waited and the elevator door opened. In walked the man from 12G, whom we called "Shrek" because he looked like the cartoon ogre and smelled like rot.

A couple of weeks earlier, I had been waiting on our floor for the elevator to come. The doors opened and Shrek, clad only in yellowed boxer shorts, ran out and up the staircase. I got in and didn't breathe through my nose. When I went to press L, I noticed it was lit, as was the button for every other floor. HE PRESSED ALL THE BUTTONS! This grown man. What the hell kind of crap was that? Paul didn't want me to ride the elevator alone anymore after that.

So, in the laundry room, I waited as he took forEVER to empty the washer. He'd remove one item, shake it, lumber over and place it in the dryer. Then he'd walk back and do it again. I sighed loudly, and then I saw his feet. Where toes should have been there were bloody stumps. I looked at his face and saw that he wore glasses as thick and dirty as subway windows and that his body was covered in bruises and scabs. He finally left, and I sat considering sending my wash out. A woman I was friendly with who'd been in the building for twenty years came in with her baskets. I asked her if she knew what the story was with 12G.

"Oh, yeah, he's on disability," she said, and wrinkled her nose. "He has diabetes."

Of course—the vision loss, the cuts not healing, the excess weight, and the circulation problems in the feet. I started to feel weak, thinking about the same thing happening to Paul if we didn't get his diabetes under control.

"Do you know his name?" I asked her.

"William," she said.

William. I couldn't call him Shrek anymore, even in my head.

Eight

The Cow for Free

"I FEEL SO SAD," I said, looking out at the barren trees of Central Park from Margot's office. She waited for me to continue.

"You know, I feel like my life should be a romantic comedy and it's turning into the kind of German existentialist film I hate."

Margot nodded. "It's certainly been hard."

"Oh, did I tell you about Paul's brother?"

She shook her head no.

"Paul left work yesterday to take him to the hospital. He has kidney stones. I met them over at Beth Israel."

Paul's brother Dave had been living in Paul's old apartment on Avenue A.

I was feeling my eyes stinging. I never cried, but I felt like I was about to.

"Can you say what's going through your mind?"

"I'm really mad," I said, the tears coming on. "How the hell did I get in the middle of this shit? This is not supposed to be my life."

Margot didn't respond. We both knew all about the life of leisure I had been promised by my mother. I didn't even want that anymore. I just wanted to stop feeling like I was living under a ladder made of broken mirrors . . . with a large black cat sitting on top whose name was Thirteen.

"You have a very good relationship," Margot said as I was leaving. "And a very good job."

When I got in to work that day, I found out that along with the rest of the staff at *Pop-Up*, I'd been nominated for an Emmy Award for Outstanding Special Class Writing. From this day forth, no matter what happened, I would have "Emmy-nominated writer" attached to my name. Finally, an event my mother could sink her teeth into. I would need a gown, shoes and a purse, new makeup, highlights, a haircut . . . It wasn't a wedding, but you wouldn't know by us.

NOT ONLY wasn't it a wedding, it wasn't even a bar mitzvah. Held in a banquet room in the Marriott Marquis, the Daytime Craft Service Award ceremony was the unattractive, overweight, asthmatic child of award shows. There was a buffet table with hot plates and Sterno cans. I got more excited by my high school prom. And we lost to the broadcast of the Macy's Thanksgiving Day Parade.

A few weeks later, I no longer had a good job, either. The details are murky, but it seems that Paul's and my relationship was not good for morale at the office. I had slept my way right out of a job.

A few days later I met with Lauren Zalaznick, the executive in charge of production at VH1, who started e-mailing people before I left her office, and by the time I got home I had a job on a music-video game show. It wasn't due to start for a couple of months, which gave me time to cry a lot. I started wearing my hair in two braids because I felt it made me look more pitiable, like Andrew Wyeth's Helga.

In the interim I got a work-for-hire job. I would earn ten thousand bucks for writing a six-book series on World War II for junior high students. And I had six weeks to write them.

Sitting on the floor of our apartment with books and maps and first-person accounts spread all over the floor, I tried to comprehend something, anything. I made charts and timelines, anything to make sense of what I was doing. Otto would walk into the room and lie down in the middle of a book and I'd have to lift his ass to read about "The Sinking of *Repulse* and *Prince of Wales.*" It was the hardest thing I'd ever done—workwise.

I called Paul and said, "What do you know about World War Two?"

He replied, "I saw *Back to Bataan* and *The Bridge on the River Kwai.*"

"That's it?

"Yeah, why?"

"Because I don't get this!"

"Get what?"

"World War Two."

"Oh." Paul's voice was steady. "Baby, I think if you're using me for a source, you're in a little trouble."

He wasn't wrong. The only ones worse off than I were the little kids who were supposed to be learning from these books. What was going to happen if I didn't get it? Would a generation of kids grow up thinking Dunkirk was a butler on a seventies sitcom? Do you know how complicated the Battle of Midway is? There are a bunch of fake-outs in it. Really, if it were meant to be understood by me, it would never have worked as a military strategy.

Toward the end of every day I'd have a panic attack. My idea was to call the editor and say I had a disease and had to quit. Or someone close to me had a disease. Or I'd just commit suicide and then I wouldn't have to do it. Or I'd pretend that I had gone crazy, and sit and rock back and forth. I looked at Otto and thought, "I'm a writer, I can figure this out." Then I begged the editor to fire me, but she wouldn't; there wasn't time to get another writer. The best they could do was have a military consultant go over what I wrote, but I'd have to pay him part of my money. I gladly handed it over.

Between what was left and a nice-sized tax refund, I had a little money in my savings and decided to approach Paul about combining our finances. I was starting to feel like Paul's poor roommate. When I didn't have enough to cover my share of the bills, I borrowed money from him. It didn't make sense. Until then, I had nothing and didn't feel right about saying, "Let's combine funds, your hundred grand and my handsome Furla checkbook cover." Now I had a little meat to put in the pot, and before it was gone I spoke my piece. Paul agreed to talk to his therapist about it, and the next thing I knew, we had joint accounts. Paul had CDs and checking and money market accounts, but no credit cards and no wallet, just a paper envelope that his bank card fit in. I, on the other hand, had thirteen cards (ATM, MasterCard, Visa, American Express, Discover, a card that my mother gave me "for emergencies," and store cards for Barneys, Bergdorf's, Bendel's, Bloomingdale's, Banana Republic, Saks, and Neiman Marcus) and a Fendi wallet that my mother got me in Rome. It was such a perfect illustration of our differences, me with all that shit and a mound of debt and Paul with his six-figure income, who could not have cared less about small fine leather goods. We had a lot to learn from each other, but all we talked about, or didn't talk about, was getting engaged.

What is it about this argument that reduces physicists and supermodels to untamed shrews? No matter how smart or confident or successful I was feeling, the ring not being on my finger, the engagement not being set, was all anything was ever about for me. We took a walk one early evening on new snow in Riverside Park, and I thought, "This would be a lovely place to be proposed to." We went to Vermont in October and I thought, "How cool would a Halloween wedding be, with jack-o-lanterns on every table."

On the phone one night Barbara asked me what my obsession was all about.

"Why are you driving yourself crazy? You know eventually you'll get married."

"I don't know, Barb. I feel like if I wait one more second I'm going to jump out a window."

"But why?" she said.

She wasn't asking why I loved Paul; anyone around us for five minutes agreed that no two people were more meant to be together. Why, though, was I obsessed with this engagement thing?

Being friends with someone from fourth grade to midlife gives you a unique perspective.

Barbara is nine months older than I am, and her sister Kristin is nine months younger. The three of us were always close, but in high school we had that intense level of friendship that only high school girls can develop.

One day they were over at my house, and Barbara was getting out of the pool, and she said, "You know what word I'm not comfortable with? 'Nuance.' It's not a real word, like 'gesture.' That's a real word. With 'gesture' you know where you stand. But 'nuance'? I don't know. Maybe I'm wrong."

"What did you say?" I said, eyes squinting in disbelief.

Barbara said, "It's a line from a movie."

"*Diner,*" I said, the way that someone might have said "Buddhism."

My mother was at the pool. "Oh boy!" She laughed. She was all too aware that during a bad bout of the flu, I had rented and renewed Barry Levinson's classic film about friends who hung out in a diner in "Baltimore, 1959." Not only had I watched it on a loop, I also stopped and started it about a thousand times so I could type out the dialogue on our thirty-pound Royal manual, transcribing parts of it and then photographing the TV set so that when I wasn't watching the movie, I could look at these horrible-quality off-the-TV photographs and read my text, consuming it like Renfield and his spiders.

"What other movies do you . . . like?" I asked.

Kristin piped up, "*Ordinary People*—"

"'It's a clean break, I think it can be saved,'" I said, recalling Mary Tyler Moore's line about the broken plate. We howled like people who find out they all came from the same Sicilian province.

"Julie also likes *Raging Bull*," my mother said, and they both cackled. We went back and forth naming titles—*Fame*, *Jaws*—and the few that we didn't have in common we were anxious to bring to one another. "I'll teach you *Dog Day Afternoon*," I offered.

What a sweet gift—how lucky I was to find two comrades who were willing to spend bucolic summer days at the house with the pool, tennis court, and horses, but spend them inside a dark room watching *Star Wars*, *The Godfather*, *Apocalypse Now*, *Annie Hall*, and *Desperately Seeking Susan*.

We traveled into Manhattan to go to "in-stores" at the Tower Records on East Fourth Street, lining up for hours to get our albums signed by Johnny Rotten or the guys from

Squeeze. We waited on line at TKTS to get half-price tickets to Broadway shows—and if there wasn't anything we liked we would just see *A Chorus Line* again. We ate a lot of doughnuts on the Metro-North commuter train. Dressed in "the castoffs of old men and bums," as my mother called our vintage clothes, we looked as big as bears, and to further distance the world we talked in a movie-quote language so inside that no one, and I mean no one, wanted to hang around us, except us.

Going to sleep at night in Barbara and Kristin's white-and-glass-wall living room, we made the pact to all live near one another in New York City when we grew up and be friends forever. So when Barbara ended up at Parsons and Kristin and I went to NYU, we lived the dream.

Maybe we all needed to separate to grow and become who we needed to, because a very minor argument at the end of my and Barbara's sophomore year escalated into a major shattering of the friendship. We didn't speak for a few years, and then, after just a few small communications, we had a total reconciliation. We would never not be friends again.

Grown-up Barbara is my hero. When she felt she was drinking too much, she stopped. When smoking got in her way, she quit. She read a book that explained how to organize finances, and got herself out of debt and into saving money. I remember sitting with her over coffee when she decided that the place she was working was not doing it for her; she thought about where she wanted to be and went there. It was like Babe Ruth pointing to the center-field bleachers and then socking a homer there. I never knew anyone who chose so many tough challenges and triumphed. A steadfast little tin soldier, she makes me so proud I could cry. I always hoped that her secure self-reliance and ability to face what's painful in the road ahead would rub off on me.

So I couldn't explain to her why I wanted to get married so badly. It was simply in my DNA.

Margot said that as long as I *wanted* to be with Paul and didn't *need* to be with him, it was fine. I complained to her more than to anyone. I felt like I couldn't tell anyone else how angry it made me to be feeling that way.

A few weeks before Christmas Paul said he had to talk to me about something. He said he wanted to get me a very "significant" gift but didn't feel comfortable about picking it out himself and wondered if he could tell me what it was, destroying the surprise but getting my input because it was something LARGE and IMPORTANT and he didn't want to get it wrong with this thing that would be around forever and cost thousands of dollars. Finally, the moment had arrived for my twinkly, sparkly ring. What should I get, emerald cut? The hot Asscher cut? I loved that one, very Art Deco.

We took the F train down to the Lower East Side, where the Smith girls' jeweler since 1929, Mr. Padrusch, had his shop. Paul must have called Mattie or my mother. I felt my legs getting shaky. I pried a Charlie Brown bandage off my left forefinger.

We got up to the street and he led me into a large warehousey storefront on Houston Street filled with a distinctive arrangement of detritus: broken stone pillars, railroad insulators, marble statues that once sat in shell fountains, and above the door a large vintage tin clock with a blue-light advertising a bygone matzoh company called Star of David. Something told me I was about to be bitterly disappointed as I was led over to a wall of antique celestial maps. I studied the titles, reading them over and over to keep from passing out. *Hæmisphærii borealis coeli et terræ sphærica scenographia . . . Planisphærium Braheum mundi totius ex hypothesi . . . Hæmisphærium stellatum Australe æquali sphærum proportione.* Ah yes, Latin, the language of disappointment.

The owner came rushing over. "This must be Julie."

God, the guy knew my name. I gave him a weak smile.

He cleared his throat. "Cellarius's 1660 *Harmonia macrocosmica,* the most beautiful and important seventeenth-century celestial atlas, is an exquisite work of art that comprehensively expresses the state of scientific knowledge of the heavens. Its spectacular illustrations of Copernican theory, along with those of Ptolemy and Brahe, are perfect examples . . ."

I smiled and nodded, while in my head I heard my mother's voice screaming, "SHADDAP, YA EGGHEAD!"

"I know, it's amazing," Paul said, misinterpreting my expression.

"They are lovely, but I need to think about it," I said, and suggested we walk over to B&H Dairy for blintzes so the day wouldn't be a total loss.

Days became weeks, weeks became months, and my sweet

patience became a really bad personality. The thoughts were always the same: "He thinks he's too good for me? Who does he think he's going to get? Kate Winslet? Liz Phair? Sandra Day O'Connor?"

Paul assured me that he was working on the issue.

"What is the issue, exactly?" I asked.

He told me something different every time I brought it up—he wasn't ready, he didn't want to be a responsible adult, and that was all part of it, but not "it." Here is the reason Paul did not want to marry me: I wasn't working.

He talked to his therapist about it, and the therapist asked him what I did for money. Paul said, "She gets it from her parents." The therapist said, "Well, think of that like her job. Not everyone gets money the same way"—i.e., lawyers, drug dealers, lobbyists, trust fund recipients all have *different ways* of getting money—"but money is money. Just look at it as her income." I didn't know this was going on at the time; I would've puked if I'd heard it. My parents weren't supporting me; they were helping me out now and again. To me it's like saying that sleeping with a guy after he buys you dinner makes you a hooker. It wasn't an arrangement.

IN THE SPRING OF 2001, Jancee called me up and said she had something to tell me. It sounded serious.

"Are you buying an antique celestial map?" I asked her.

"Close," she said. "Tom and I got engaged."

"Oh, that is so wonderful, Jance," I gushed. "He's the best guy. I love him."

"I just want you to know," she said tearfully, "that I won't enjoy this until it happens to you."

I sobbed on the phone and told her that I loved her and that she'd better enjoy it and I was going to make her bridal shower.

Then I hung up and sent cartoon daggers into Paul's chest cavity, where his heart had once been.

I had just barely gotten over Kristin's engagement in January, and now Jancee! I had begun seeing Paul long before either of them started seeing *their* fiancés!

I told Paul the news, seething.

"Maybe we can go pick out a ring," Paul said, resigned.

The next day we went to a private jeweler on Fifth Avenue and picked out a stone and a setting. I knew exactly what I wanted and I didn't want to go too crazy. It just had to be bigger than my sister-in-law's, like my grandmother would've wanted.

I called Mattie and told her that it was two carats, and very white. She yelled at me. "You could've gone to Padrusch and gotten a big yellow Jew diamond for half the price!"

A funny thing happened when we left the jeweler: Paul felt great relief and I wanted to leave town—alone. All the time I'd been pushing and pushing, I hadn't been thinking about what it was that I wanted and what it meant, only that I couldn't have it. Paul, on the other hand, had been doing a tremendous amount of genuine soul-searching and was set to go.

Fortunately, I had a few months to adjust. Though the

ring was ready the week after we picked it out, he wasn't ready to give it to me. I didn't know what the hell was happening. I started to get mad all over again.

September 1, 2001, was a beautiful day. We sat by the water in Riverside Park and watched the boats. When we got home Paul turned on the TV—as luck would have it, both the Yankees and the Mets were playing. He was switching back and forth between the games when I said for the ten millionth time, "Today would be a nice day to get engaged."

"Okay," Paul said.

I looked at him, waiting for the punch line. There wasn't one. He romantically muted the TV, dug through his underwear drawer, and pulled out a green leather ring box with a matching satin ribbon.

"What?" I said. *What?*

He gave me the box and I opened it and there was my ring.

"Will you marry me?" Paul said.

"Mmmmmmm . . . okay," I answered. Then he turned off the TV and we didn't call anyone. It was my first act as Paul's wife-to-be. I didn't call my mother.

After having dinner at an overpriced local fish place, a meal that neither of us tasted, we walked home. The final item on the menu was a brilliant starry sky, the kind you don't normally get in Manhattan, and a sliver of a ginger moon.

"Can we go up to the roof?" I asked.

The top of our building had a spectacular view of the city, the Hudson, and the night sky.

"Ask me again," I said under the stars, "so I don't have to tell our grandchildren about muting the Yankees game."

"Yankees and Mets," Paul corrected. "Will you marry me?" he asked again.

"Yes," I said.

He smiled and kissed me. "You know you're going to tell the TV-muting story, because it's much more entertaining."

"No I won't," I said, but of course I did. Margot said the men who rented white horses and suits of armor for their proposal usually ended up being all show and no substance and this low-key proposal showed much more promise.

"Finally!" my mother said. Mattie and my cousin Stephanie took me to lunch at the Four Seasons Hotel. We all looked at my ring over and over. Paul's mother was happy, too, but she was a little distracted. She'd had a sore throat and cough since Mother's Day, and a litany of tests done near her home in Newburgh were inconclusive. She was scheduled to see a specialist. Her appointment was for September 15, at the Manhattan Eye, Ear and Throat Hospital.

Immediately Paul and I started scheduling times to look at venues for our wedding. For nine blissful days we were engaged. On September 11 we had an appointment at the Waldorf-Astoria. It was expensive, but we wanted to check it out, just for the hell of it. For obvious reasons, we never got there.

Mattie called me and told me to turn the TV on. A plane had hit the World Trade Center. As we were watching, Mattie gasped. Another one had hit. My mind went to a virus in the computerized navigational system of the air traffic controllers. We went up to the roof of the building, where nine days before we'd had our romantic reproposal, and watched as the towers collapsed. Everyone talks about the weather that day; it seemed impossible that the world could be coming to an end under such a glorious sky.

That day the guy from the Waldorf left two messages. He wanted to make sure we were okay (the first message), and then, later, wanted to know when we would like to reschedule our appointment. There was something oddly comforting about the fact that this guy was still working on his quota.

In the next few days we smelled the smoke and talked about what we should do. After a bomb threat at Penn Station, I begged Paul to get us out of New York, but the bridges into and out of the city were closed. Along Riverside Park, the Henry Hudson Parkway, normally buzzing, was as quiet as a country road. Above our heads was only the sound of military jets; the weather continued to be way too nice.

Each evening Paul and I tuned in to the now familiar press conference with the fire commissioner, Thomas Von Essen, police chief Bernard Kerik, and Mayor Rudy Giuliani. One night when a reporter asked a question, Giuliani nodded, signaling he would take it.

"Has anyone ever told you you look like Mike Mussina, the pitcher for the Yankees?" Giuliani, a rabid Yankees fan, asked the reporter.

The reporter mumbled a no, but Giuliani continued, "You really do. You really look like him."

Paul and I looked at each other and erupted with laughter.

It was such a brilliantly natural and ordinary thing to say. I wasn't nuts about the mayor before, but then I wanted to leap into the TV and hug him and his big Giuliani comb-over.

We were all anxious to get back to normal. Paul's mother was waiting for planes to fly again because the specialist she was supposed to see had been on vacation in Florida during the terrorist attack.

When he came back, she went in and had a biopsy done on her lymph nodes. When the results came in, she was told to go to Sloan-Kettering to decide how to proceed. I must say that despite our recent spate of bad luck, I was sure it was nothing and that she'd be fine. Jean Leo-Herlihy kicked ass in Talbot's slacks and snowman sweaters. There was something very Nancy Pelosi about her.

After losing Paul's father, Roger, suddenly when she was forty, Paul's mother went to work, with two sons at home and two in college. She started attending Parents Without Partners, where three years later she met another man, whom she would marry. Ten years later he was diagnosed with cancer, and he passed away soon after. She picked herself up once more, went to church every day, volunteered with Habitat for Humanity and at a soup kitchen. Her beloved sister, Josephine, died of cancer, and she would eventually bury both her parents. From where I sat, that had been *enough*. Maybe it felt that way to her, too, and that's why she didn't visit Paul in the hospital.

Paul went with her to Sloan to review the test results, but they hadn't come in. When they phoned, they found the tests hadn't been sent: 9/11 had wreaked havoc on the mail system, and things just sat. Since she'd come all the way down from Newburgh, she didn't want to reschedule, so she and Paul went to Manhattan Eye, Ear and Throat, which wasn't all that far away. They picked up the results and carried them to Sloan. The plan was then to come back to our apartment, where I'd have dinner ready.

I stood in my kitchen feeling agitated as it got later and later. The dinner I'd prepared for my mother-in-law-to-be was getting more and more dried out. I called my mother to ask her if I should take the chicken out of the oven or leave it in on low; I got her machine. In the end, everything was overcooked, except, by some cruel joke, the roasted baby red potatoes, which were undone, potatoes al dente. The broccoli was hay, the rosemary ciabatta rolls desiccated lumps from being reheated. I obsessed over the arid dinner. I should have made Italian food. Safe, comforting, moist. And for dessert, I had biscotti. Why didn't I just serve everyone a big bowl of sand?

The door finally opened and Paul came in carrying his mother's overnight bag, his eyes red from crying. Jean looked at the ground as she came in. I started talking fast and ushering them to the table. We choked down the food—no one was very hungry, but we ate mechanically. I was trying to make it so no one would have to tell me what happened. Keep passing, talking, getting butter. Then Jean cleared her throat.

"It's bad."

I nodded, not wanting her to have to go on.

Paul continued: "It's non-Hodgkin's lymphoma."

I didn't know what that meant, but it sounded like non-Hodgkin's should be good. I was wrong.

"I'll call Matt and he can call his father-in-law." This was Lara's father, Dr. Jim Cox, head of radiation oncology at M. D. Anderson Cancer Center in Houston.

"That would be good," Jean said.

"I'll call him tonight."

"Thank you," Paul said.

Jean excused herself to the bathroom and Paul told me quietly that Jean's cancer was Stage IV. He referred to a rumpled piece of paper, on which I recognized his doodles.

"Stage I is early and the disease is limited to a small area, while Stage IV disease is more widespread. It's also called 'late-stage disease.' The more widespread the disease, the harder it may be to treat the cancer." His hands and voice were shaky. I hugged him and kissed him, then picked up the phone to call Matt.

"Jim's in Tokyo, but I'll e-mail him tonight," Matt said. "I know he'll be glad to help." I love my brother.

The following week I was watching CNN when there was a breaking story. A woman was in critical condition in a Manhattan hospital, where she was being treated for a suspected case of inhaled anthrax, the most serious form of the infection. This was the first suspected case of anthrax in New York. The newscaster went on to describe the patient, a sixty-one-year-old woman who worked in a storage supply area near the mailroom of the Manhattan Eye, Ear and Throat Hospital. The woman might have handled mail as part of her work, and the hospital would be closed while about three hundred employees were being interviewed and, if necessary, put on a course of antibiotics. Anyone who'd been there in that time period blah, blah, blah. I started sweating. How was this possible? This was the kind of news I automatically ignored; like winning lottery numbers, it didn't apply to me. Except that Paul and Jean had been there during that very time period, to pick up her records. He'd described the records room as "a dingy place, in the basement, way at the end of a long maze of hallways." They were there for half an hour, waiting for a guy to dig out the files, during which time Jean had felt very ill with no place to sit. I called Paul at work to let him know and told him I'd call our doctor.

My whole life had operated within a system of beliefs that held that everything worked out or could be fixed. If there were questions about health, we called my cousin Barry, the doctor; legal questions, my cousin Jimmy. Financial problems, my grandfather would give us money. When some crazy was buzzing my door on Eightieth Street, I called the police and they came and dealt with it. When the downstairs neighbor fell asleep with a lit joint, the fire department responded.

Now a figurative asteroid had come and smashed my protected planet to bits, shredding all of the safety nets. Whom could I call about the terrorists? The police? The army? The president? Could my grandma buy Al Qaeda and fire bin Laden? What about my fiancé's only living parent and her almost certain death sentence? Should I write a letter to Oprah's Angel Network?

What doesn't kill you makes you stronger; but, I was finding, there could be a significant lag time between not dying and being able to move mountains.

Nine

Can We Register for Rent Money?

MARGOT USED TO KNOW immediately if I was depressed because I'd spend whole weeks of sessions talking about Disney movies.

"You know what I want to know about Sleeping Beauty?" I'd ask her. She'd quietly wait for me to tell her. "What's she going to *do* all day?"

I'd look back at her from the couch to see what she was doing.

"And Cinderella, and Snow White, and Belle, and Ariel."

"Can you say more?"

"Well, they all have very clear purposes before they meet their princes—housework, cooking, cleaning, sleeping, or swimming—but after, I just can't see it."

"What do you imagine?"

"I imagine them walking around the castle, thinking, What the hell am I supposed to do now?"

I would think about all of this because I was watching the movies so often—from the minute I woke up till I left the house, and again upon my return—so holes were bound to appear. My quirky habit was not limited to Disney princess pictures, though I did tend to favor their endings (happy). I watched Fred Astaire and Ginger Rogers movies for the same reasons. Depending on the issue I was struggling with, I might be watching *Close Encounters of the Third Kind*; *Field of Dreams*; *Dog Day Afternoon*; *Reds*; *Dick Tracy*; *Paper Moon*; *The Gay Divorcee*; *Empire of the Sun*; *Now, Voyager*; *All the President's Men*; *E.T.*; or the very beginning of *Pinocchio*, until the end of Jiminy Cricket's singing "When You Wish upon a Star."

Little kids will watch a movie this way, ten times a day every day (or as often as a bigger person will permit them), until they can recite the whole thing. The repetition is comforting. I would turn a movie on when I got up in the morning, then shower, dress, put on makeup, and eat breakfast with it running as background music. I was drawn to a familiar world that was entirely predictable and had nothing to do with me, until I brought it up in therapy. Then, suddenly, I was a part of it.

Once Paul and I moved in together, I couldn't do that. The apartment was no longer my personal movie theater. It was the lone thing I missed about my singlehood.

With Jean in heavy-duty chemo, which involved our

sharing the task of taking her to appointments with Bob and his wife, Debbye, and having her stay at our or their home, and with the city in post-9/11 freak-out mode, I was in deep need of some escapism. I thought about taking up drinking, and I might have if it didn't make me feel so dehydrated and crummy. I felt like I could really get behind a good addiction, and no one would blame me, but I was asthmatic, which ruled out cigarettes and pot, and I was already hyper, so forget about cocaine. I'd seen heroin addicts on the subway, and they were too scary, nodding off and calling out and drooling—seemed like a good way to get your pocket picked, too. I Googled "street drugs" and started perusing the White House's informational webpage. It looked like any Internet store except without the little shopping cart symbols.

- 4-MTA (4-methylthio-amphetamine)
- Alpha-ethyltryptamine
- Amphetamine
- Amyl nitrite
- Benzocaine
- Club drugs
- Cocaine
- Crack cocaine
- Depressants
- Designer drugs
- Dimethyltryptamine
- Ecstasy (methylene-dioxymethamphetamine; MDMA)
- Fentanyl
- Gamma hydroxy-butyrate (GHB)
- GBL (gamma butyrolactone)
- GHB (gamma hydroxybutyrate)
- Hallucinogens
- Hashish
- Heroin
- Inhalants

- Isobutyl nitrite
- Ketamine
- Lidocaine
- LSD (lysergic acid diethylamide)
- Mannitol
- Marijuana
- MDMA (methylene-dioxymethamphetamine)
- Mescaline
- Methadone
- Methamphetamine
- Methaqualone
- Methcathinone
- Methylene-dioxymethamphetamine (MDMA)
- Methylphenidate (Ritalin)
- Morphine
- Narcotics
- Nexus
- Nicotine
- Nitrous oxide
- Opium
- Oxycodone
- OxyContin
- PCP (phencyclidine)
- Peyote
- Phenobarbital
- Procaine
- Psilocybin/psilocin
- Ritalin
- Rohypnol
- Scopolamine
- Speed
- Steroids
- Stimulants
- Strychnine
- Sudafed
- Talwin

I recalled from Matt's *New York Times Magazine* piece on Ecstasy that what intrigued me most was that the tablets had all these different pictures on them: a yin and yang, the Calvin Klein logo, the ubiquitous happy face. I read the White House's descriptions of the effects, and none of them claimed to make you feel as though you were sitting through forty continuous hours of *Indiana Jones and the Last Crusade.* So I deleted "street drugs" and typed in "wedding dresses." I found site after site of not just dresses but bouquets, photographers, and venues. And very quickly, within minutes, I got hooked.

Ah, the modern marketing world of weddings. I had watched numerous brides dip varying amounts of their toes into this water, some barely getting moist, others requiring scuba gear.

I thought I could do it sensibly enough: my mother and Mattie and I would buzz around to a bunch of places and in a couple of days the whole thing would be planned. I forgot about who I was marrying. Except for the elements that had to do specifically with my appearance, Paul was interested in everything. Every part that had to do with the wedding, we did *together.* I called my friend Leslie, who single-handedly oversaw the production of her own wedding, the most spectacular I'd ever been to.

She got out her files and went through her lists.

I'd alternately bark "I don't need that" and "I don't want that," while she good-naturedly assured me that whatever I did would be fine and would be my own.

"Paul's and my own," I reminded her.

"Right," she said quickly. "It'll be great."

A couple of weeks after we got engaged, we went up to my parents' "new" house on the New York–Vermont border. The modern passive-solar house on 175 acres with a swimming pond and cross-country ski trails was my father's dream. The nearby town made Katonah look like Las Vegas. Though the rest of the world was mired in 9/11 news, my parents' local newspaper had stories about a "skunk whisperer" and the local man "who invented disco." It was a fabulous trip courtesy of the bad news censors. What a perfect place for my dad—a man who wouldn't watch a movie without being assured of its happy ending—to live in. Who could blame him? He'd grown up in a horror movie. He'd had enough.

And the topics of conversation that weekend at the house they called "Ganaden"—Hebrew for Garden of Eden—ran from wedding talk to wedding talk. If my mother and I had to pay a penny for every time we said the words "wedding," "hair," "makeup," "shoes," "dress," and "flowers," we would both be destitute. It was really lucky for me I was there, because the only person in the world who isn't bored by endless bride-talk is the mother of the bride. I remember being at Brian's for Cheryl's bridal shower, when one morning she came into the kitchen laughing.

"You know what I just realized?" she said, eager to reveal the epiphany.

I looked at her expectantly.

"Last time you were here it was six months before my wedding. And now it's two months before my wedding!"

I looked at my mother, waiting for her to heap abuse on Cheryl for this pronouncement. She was speechless, so I asked Cheryl if the ring was squeezing her brain. She could connect any topic to her upcoming wedding, from the War of 1812 to plumbing fixtures to Matt's high school friend who was having surgery on his deviated septum.

Now it was my turn. And being the only daughter and the last child to marry, my mother was breaking down the stable door to gallop a victory lap with me. The two of us were so hepped up on wedding shit that when we drove over to Manchester, Vermont, to do a little outlet shopping, we bought me a bridal gown.

The Nicole Miller store had only a handful of white dresses tucked away in a corner, but our radar homed right in on them. They were samples used in a summer fashion show at a local garden club, and they were for sale. I plucked out one; it was like Gwyneth Paltrow's *Emma* gown. I imagined myself wearing it with bare feet and flowers in my hair. The price was $135, further reduced because it had some soiling on the hem. No matter, I thought in a tidy British accent, madrigals playing in my head.

We left the shop and I stood in the parking lot, joy melting to near tears.

"Let's just go," I uttered.

Crestfallen, we barely spoke the first fifteen minutes of the drive.

"Why do I feel so deflated?" I said to the road ahead.

"Because it's over!" my mother intuited. "We were supposed to go to Vera Wang and Barneys and Bergdorf's and Saks and Carolina Herrera and have a nice girly lunch!"

"I know!" I said, like we'd both been cruelly set up. "I liked the dress okay, but it took, like, two seconds!"

"There were no choices, not even one other style," Mom said, perking up. "And it's dirty!"

We both knew at that moment that this was not going to be the end of the wedding dress.

"We can't return it, you know," I said cautiously.

"No one says you're definitely not going to wear it," she said, as if my father were in earshot. "We'll keep it as a backup, and if, after we go to Vera Wang and Barneys and Bergdorf's and Saks and Carolina Herrera, you decide that it's the one for you, then great."

"Princess Diana had, like, four dresses."

"Japanese women do that, too. Mattie showed us that Japanese movie star's wedding, remember?"

"I think the four Diana had were the same."

"Oh, like in case she got cocktail sauce on it?"

"Yeah, or mustard from a pig in a blanket."

We chuckled.

"I just can't imagine that after seeing those immense designer duchesse satin and Byzantium empire brocade and hand-beaded Indian lace gowns, I'm going to want this"—and I picked up the bag and looked at the gown's label—"100% polyester."

My mother looked at me with Norma Rae defiance. "No way in HELL my baby's wearing a polyester dress."

"No way," I echoed. "I bet I can sell it on eBay."

"It was a hundred and ten dollars!" she said, a hint of outrage in her voice. "I don't care if you throw it in the garbage."

We went into our own heads for a few minutes and I started to feel guilty. "Who knows?" I said, worrying about my karma, "maybe I won't find anything I like better."

"Maybe," she said, pulling her Saab into an autumn farm stand.

LATER THAT DAY my mother made loads of calls to her cousins, one of whom started spewing advice about florists. Ooh, that pissed her off.

"I don't know how to pick out nice flowers?" she said when she hung up the phone. "Dina told me to give the florist 'key words.' She said when Allison, her fat toad, got married she told the florist to make the arrangements 'lavish and whimsical.'" Mom was past indignant.

Paul chimed in: "We want *our* flowers to be 'cheap and menacing.'"

"Yeah," I said. "When I walk down the aisle, I want people to squinch up their faces and wonder, 'Who died in the bride's bouquet?'"

Up at my parents' house we were sharing the guest amenities with Aunt Suzie and Uncle Harris. My father had only one sibling, his sister, Suzie, who at fifteen years his junior was more like a daughter. She and Harris had lived near us in Katonah with their two kids, Jonny and Mandi, and then, when my parents moved up to Granville, they bought an inn near Killington, Vermont.

After a few years in the inn business, people tend to burn out, so they decided to sell and move to a house that they would build. During the end stages of construction, when things were inevitably delayed, they stayed with my parents. That was where Suzie was when she first fell from a standing position at the kitchen sink. When she started to feel numbness, they took her to a doctor.

The grave suspicion was that what Suzie had been experiencing was the beginning stage of ALS (amyotrophic lateral sclerosis, or Lou Gehrig's disease). ALS is a progressive neurodegenerative disease that affects nerve cells in the brain and spinal cord. Motor neurons reach from the brain to the spinal cord and from the spinal cord to the muscles throughout the body. When the motor neurons die, the ability of the brain to initiate and control muscle movement is lost. With voluntary muscle action progressively affected, patients in the later stages of the disease may become totally paralyzed. In most cases, their minds remain unaffected. The progressive degeneration eventually leads to death.

We'd seen it already. My father's mother had died from it, and while it wasn't necessarily hereditary, Suzie had a medical history almost identical to Grandma Billie's, and the same blood type. The initial tests were inconclusive, but soon after the diagnosis was heartbreakingly confirmed.

Paul and I asked Suzie and Harris to read a poem at our wedding, and prayed that she would be there.

A few weeks later, Mom came into New York. The endless river of crud was taking its toll on everyone, and there was a lot riding on this day to be great. Together with Mattie, my matron of honor, we went to find The Dress.

If there's ever a princess moment in the life of a normal gal—not a debutante or a child of royalty or a Best Actress nominee—it's trying on her wedding dress. In an upscale salon, surrounded by gowns and mirrors and tiaras and people waiting on you, there is a moment of intoxication when words like "birthright" come to mind and you find yourself speaking more genteelly, and standing straighter.

For me, it began at our first stop, Vera Wang Bridal Salon, the legendary Upper East Side dresser of brides great and small.

After giving your information to reception, a sales associate heralds you upstairs and begins asking some general questions about style and price range. I looked out the window onto Madison Avenue and thought about the countless number of times I'd gone by here on foot, in a bus, in a cab, and looked up, wondering what it would feel like to be *the bride*. I found my thoughts wandering, uncomfortably, to a striking blond woman I'd seen on the news whose fiancé was buried in the rubble of the World Trade Center, and who told the reporter, with absolute certainty, that they would find him, he would be okay, they would be married.

It's not that I wasn't in the spirit of the celebration. On the contrary, I felt that everyone needed happy occasions. Margot, who'd experienced loss in her own life, was very adamant about the need to give close friends and relatives a good reason to come together.

So many women tell you they bought the first dress they tried on, and if it had been a lower price, I, too, would've bought the first dress I tried on. It was incredible, and it was

$5,600, without alterations, veil, shoes, undergarments, or the tiara I decided I was wearing. This was on the lower end of the price scale, where dresses went up to six figures. I wanted to go over the top, but without exceeding the budget of a developing country. My mother's wheels were spinning—she wanted so much to give me what I wanted—but it was just too much. We were looking at at least $7,000 for my outfit alone.

"Thank you," I said to the sales associate. "Let's go," I said to my mother and Mattie.

I walked on ahead of them down Madison, toward Bergdorf's, our next stop. "What the hell am I doing?" I thought. This is turning into a terrible day. My mother feels sad, Mattie feels sad, and I feel like I'm doing something wrong. It started to rain and we stopped under an awning to regroup.

"I don't think I want to go to Bergdorf's," I said. The truth was, I didn't want to go to any more high-end places, not even just for the experience of it. I didn't want to break my mother's heart.

"Maybe we can do it," she said, and bit her lower lip. She was talking about the seven grand.

Mattie was quiet, looking down Madison.

"I don't want it, Mom," I said, honestly. "I don't need it."

"If you say you have the polyester dress as a backup I'm going to throw myself in traffic," she said.

"Isn't there something between a hundred-dollar dress and a ten-thousand-dollar dress?" Mattie said, firmly in her troubleshooting mode.

"I don't care about the dress, really. I'm marrying the

person I love more than anyone in the world, and that's what's important to me," I said.

"You're a good girl, Julie," Mattie said, rubbing my arm.

My mother looked away, but tears were spilling down her face. I needed to do something to make this better. I remembered that there had been a discount bridal shop on Broadway near my old apartment that expanded and moved downtown. Mattie called information on her cell phone and we got directions. The place, located in the Garment District, was formerly a warehouse. The dirty tiled floor packed with circular racks of plastic-covered dresses brought me right back to my Loehmann's days. Dazzling fluorescent lighting made the blue-white gowns glow like science projects.

"There's so much here!" Mattie said excitedly. "You're definitely going to find something!"

Thank God she was there. I felt ashamed at how depressed the joint made me. My mother crossed her arms, her Versace-outlet purse falling on the floor, the contents scattering.

Like a warm wind, a young saleswoman with waist-length auburn hair in a ponytail swept in and started picking everything up. She was a charming, adorable Georgian (Soviet, not southern) girl who enveloped us like a fairy godmother. She said her name was Nadia as she led us into a dressing room, stopping along the way to compliment my mother's shoes (Mom: "I got them in Rome!") and tell me in a stage whisper that with my shape I could wear any style dress, even the skinnies!

Our spirits lifted as we sat in a dressing room littered with pins, describing the Vera Wang dress and its overwhelming price tag.

"And the saleswoman wasn't even nice!" Mattie added.

"I take care of you!" Nadia said, marching out and returning a few minutes later with several fine candidates—and a winner. I tried it on, slammed down my gavel, and said, "Sold!" Mattie and my mother were sobbing, so I knew I had it right. At $2,300, we thought we were getting a steal.

Over salad niçoise and white-wine spritzers at Café Un Deux Trois, Mattie called and canceled our remaining appointments at Saks and Bergdorf's. The day was done and I needed to get back to being a commoner again.

When I talked to Lara on the phone that night and described the dress, I somewhat apologetically told her the price. Lara had knocked everyone's socks off in her stunning Vera Wang robin's-egg-blue bridal gown.

"You did the right thing!" she said. "I spent a ridiculous amount of money on my dress and it's just sitting in our basement."

In the background I heard Matt say, "I wear it sometimes."

WHILE I WAS busily Googling "green goddess calla lilies" and images of tiaras, Paul was writing a screenplay for VH1 Original Movies. He was on a leave of absence from *Pop-Up*, so we were both working from home—he on his script, I on my wedding responsibilities. Occasionally we swapped, and I would help him with his script and he'd go out for the day, checking out reception sites. Foolishly, we thought getting married in Manhattan could be done within my father's considerable budget. It could if we were willing to do a wedding on a Wednesday at 11:15. But a Saturday-night wedding in any of the places we liked was out of the question. In order to make enough money, venues required a minimum number of people for an affair, usually between 200 and 350. Then they get to what's included per person, and you find that in no time you are so consumed by the details of entrées and flaming desserts and favors that you have no idea how you ever filled your life before you were planning this wedding. Which is what happened to me. By the time Paul proposed, I'd already made my list of eight bridesmaids (Jancee, Barbara, Kristin, Leslie, Lara, Cheryl, my NYU-film-student-turned-doctor friend Vesna, and my cousin Mandi) plus Mattie; the flower girls, my heavenly nieces Sadie and Lily and Hanah; Leslie's sweet daughter Ruby; and my beloved Sadie Resnick, Adam's daughter; plus the people we wanted to participate by reading at the wedding (my adorable neighbor from Eightieth Street, John Smith; Paul's and my friend Lisa Heller; Barbara and Kristin's mother, Dot; Suzie and Harris; and Bob Leo).

And yet there was no such thing as "being done" with the planning, because, as with Christmas shopping, you can always find just one more thing to get or do or make. Favors! Favors? Like a birthday party loot bag, people like to have a keepsake from the wedding, and a hangover doesn't count. We went from "no way" to hunting the globe for Italian

LunaStelle candies (they went with our "paper moon" wedding theme), on which we then stuck printed name labels to double as place cards; we used a moon cutout stamp to decorate the tag. I digress to make a point. One minute you're thinking about how much you love *Harry Potter and the Goblet of Fire,* and the next you're thinking, "We should do a reading from *Harry Potter and the Goblet of Fire*," and then "We should give *Harry Potter and the Goblet of Fire* as a favor," and finally "I wonder who does J. K. Rowling's hair color? Her blond is perfect. I should find out and use them for my wedding." And thus you become infected with cuckoo bride brain. There is no cure, save a hammer to the head, and it gets much worse (needing-pills worse) before it gets better.

I remember feeling very sensible when I turned down an invitation to a preview movie screening at Radio City Music Hall because I wanted to work on breaking in my wedding shoes every night. In other words, walking around my apartment *in my shoes* . . . instead of seeing a free movie at Radio City. What an ass! No one was more surprised by my behavior than I was. I wondered if I would've been so bride-brained if Jean hadn't been sick, if New York hadn't been attacked, if I'd had a job.

At the gentle urging of my parents, Paul and I checked out some reception spots in Saratoga Springs, forty-five minutes from their home. My parents were patrons of SPAC, the Saratoga Performing Arts Center, and were in love with their caterer, Angelo. So, for Angelo, we looked at a few places that his company had connections with. The place we found was from out of a dream.

Canfield Casino, a spectacular nineteenth-century ballroom, casino, and bar, had been a frequent stomping ground of Diamond Jim Brady and Lillian Russell in their day. Functioning as a museum and a site for swank parties, Canfield was also used as an old-timey location for the movie *Seabiscuit*. With Tiffany-glass windows and a ceiling that was decorated with zodiac constellations not unlike the ancient celestial maps, the place had us at hello. They had exactly one date available the following year, the Saturday of Labor Day weekend, August 31, 2002. Three hundred and sixty-four days after we got engaged. Well, we did say we weren't going to wait a whole year.

Through the endless activities related to the wedding, but having nothing to do with the marriage, a small voice somewhere in the corner of my French-braided mind could not help asking what was going to happen after.

I noticed several ads for a class at my gym called "Buff Brides"—a twelve-week stomach-flattening, arm-tightening preparation for the big day. It wasn't lost on me that they didn't offer Buff Grooms. I didn't take the class because I was already working out so much that I was looking more butch than buff. I spent fortunes on buttery highlights and frequent trims. And after a lifetime of looking at the world through thick Harold Lloyd–style spectacles, I went for laser eye surgery. Many of the revelations following upon this miraculous operation came in my shower, where I found a shaving blind spot, a little soul patch on the back of my leg, and that what I'd mistaken for marbleized grout in my shower tiles was in fact mold.

The wedding day came, and though rain had been predicted, we got miles and miles of late-August sun. It's the time of year I find the sun loveliest; its lowness in the sky is more golden and sad, like the last evening kickball games of summer vacation.

I looked around, my heart about ready to jump out of my chest. I saw the giant paper moon that Paul and my father had made and the midnight-blue velvet backdrop that my mother had made, with foil stars that I pinned on. I looked at Leslie, who had been keeping my tiara and veil straight on my head all night; Mattie, who held my hand through a million bad days; Barbara, who made paper-moon invitations; all the rest of her family, whom I loved; Vesna, who traveled from Oregon; Jancee, who after I put my dress on and had to pee offered to wipe for me if I couldn't reach under my voluminous skirts. My mother-in-law, brothers and brothers-in-law, sisters-in-law, aunts, cousins, old friends—the Goodhues, and my two favorite teachers from high school, Gil Freeman and Peggy Montgomery—Paul's friends, whom I was just beginning to love. There was a glow in the room, and I wasn't the only one who saw it. Paul and I were finally married. How could it get any better?

Ten

In Sickness, for Poorer, for Worse

Driving home to the city with a backseat full of wedding gifts, and our own gifts to each other—apple orchard cider doughnuts—I stared out the window.

"This sucks," I offered. "I'm so depressed. It's over."

Good soul that he is, Paul hardly even took it personally.

"Never again will I be a beautiful princess in a ball gown," I sighed. "It's downhill from here."

I twirled my hand in the sunlight. "At least I have this bauble," I said, referring to my new wedding ring, made of diamonds from my mother's and grandmother's original bands.

"Thanks, baby," Paul said, patting my leg, reaching behind me for the oil-speckled brown-paper doughnut bag, the diabetic's version of a bottle of Dom Pérignon. "That makes me feel so good."

"Don't you know what I mean, though? It's over! Aren't you a little depressed?"

"I'm the happiest I've ever been in my whole life," Paul said simply.

I rolled my eyes. "Give me a break."

Fortunately, Paul didn't open the passenger door and shove me out. I continued outlining for him that, yes, we received lavish gifts, yes, we were going to Italy for three weeks for our honeymoon, and yes, when we got back we were going to start trying to have a baby, which we both were dying for. None of that was the point. Now I was in the after.

There was also another development. After Paul had finished his movie, he would be out of work. I was out of work. I wasn't terribly worried about it; Paul was an eight-time Emmy nominee and beloved by VH1. When we returned from Italy, we decided, he would get a job and I'd get freelance work and together we'd pay our bills and, hopefully, get pregnant.

The honeymoon in Italy was arranged for six weeks after the wedding so we'd have a little downtime after all the excitement. I had never been to Italy, so I wanted to see a lot of it; Paul had been there as a student and was anxious to go again as a grown person. One of his great regrets the first time around was not being able to see his family in Avellino, so we were going to do that for sure.

If I were to list my shortcomings that don't involve my

appearance, I'd have to say that number one is my chronic anxiety. If Paul were to list my faults, his number one would be my need for comfort. In fact a lot of people (not related to me) have commented over the course of my life about my inability to suffer silently, or suffer at all. I give you this: Continuously plucking a person out of every uncomfortable situation does not a resilient person make!

Other than the Barbados fiasco, Paul and I had never taken a trip together. And unless you count visiting my grandfather's retirement community and several of the Club Meds, I hadn't taken many trips without him, either. Paul, on the other hand, had hitchhiked through Italy, Spain, Germany, Sweden, Norway, Denmark, Holland, Belgium, East Germany, England, France, Luxembourg, Portugal, Guatemala, and Yukon Territory, and he'd worked on a salmon boat in Alaska. (BUT he's NEVER been to FLORIDA!) Paul was a bit worried about taking me away so far from Otto and the gym and Balance Bars, and I was, too. We figured if we arranged to go with comfort as a goal, we'd do okay. We did this by enlisting the help of a travel agent whose logo should have been hundred-dollar bills with wings on them because the entire trip was punctuated with needless wastes of money.

I think there is nothing more boring, apart from hearing about someone else's dream, than getting someone else's vacation stories or pictures. I'll save the story for the grandkids, but let me just say I didn't earn any stripes on this tour.

At three weeks, the trip was too long. We started in Venice, then went to Tuscany (including Florence), Rome, Naples (with a day trip to the nearby town of Venticano), Positano on the Amalfi Coast, then back to Rome to fly home. As a kickoff, our travel agent had put us on an impossible-to-make connecting flight from Paris to Venice. So the first day of our honeymoon was spent in Charles de Gaulle Airport. It wasn't all bad, though. I invented a face there, a really big frown with angry eyebrows and a hand on my head as if I'd been smacked. The face said "I'm not having a good time at all," and it became known as Paris Face.

I felt like I should have been writing the Kvetch's Guide to Italy: there were so many disappointments. You cannot get an amazing meal for twenty bucks, as I'd heard. In fact, except for slices of pizza, we never got away with spending under sixty dollars for a meal that didn't even include wine. You have to pay for WATER; we drink a lot of water. There's no such thing as tap water there—you have a choice of bubbly in bottles or flat in bottles, and it's expensive. While three weeks is too long to go on a honeymoon, three days in each location, including travel time, is too short.

Italy is spectacular, but I am a difficult traveler. One night, we got to our hotel in Rome. It was a wreck and we were paying something like $500 a night. It claimed to have a terrace but it was under so much construction that if you opened the door, a Sahara's worth of sawdust would blow in your face. The bathroom's design scheme was "pubic hair." The room was dirty, the floor was dirty, the dirt was dirty. We'd gone looking for another hotel to move to and decided to gamble on dinner. You always hear those stories of people who drift down a cobblestone path and chance upon the best meal they ever ate. Not us. Our wanderings brought us to an English pub that served meat pies and canned green beans.

That night I lay in bed and thought about my uncle Harris, who'd been a platoon leader in Vietnam. Somewhere in my deeply troubled brain I was comparing our experiences. Me and my not yet one night in a three-star hotel after an unsatisfying dinner, and he in the malaria-ridden jungles of Da Nang and Na Trang, responsible for a troop of boys, being shot at and eating slop from a can in the hot rain. I woke Paul up to tell him my revelation, that I now kind of understood the army experience, and he looked at me and prayed out loud that this was all a dream, and went back to sleep. In the morning he gently suggested that I never utter that thought again.

We transferred to the hotel my mother had suggested—and which the travel agent had scoffed at—and it was lovely and perfect and the rest of the trip went better (not really, but I am not allowed to complain anymore). Every bit of it was worth it when we got to the small town of Venticano near Avellino and searched for Paul's relatives.

Paul's father had one brother, Ernest, who had no children. Likewise, Paul's mother's sisters, Carmella and Josephine, had had none. His family was small, but he had great hopes of discovering long-lost relatives abroad.

It was another dreary, drizzly day as we left Naples and headed past the Pompeii exit up into the hills around Avellino. Our driver was also our interpreter. When we arrived in the town, it was he who found the town council building. In communicating with the equivalent of the town clerk, we discovered that we were going to have to do better than say we were looking for the Ciarcia family. He started wildly gesticulating and repeating "Ciarcia" as he pointed to practically everyone in the office. Ciarcia, in that town, was like Smith. We needed to be more specific. I remembered someone talking about a Michelangelo Ciarcia and mentioned that name to the interpreter. Immediately the town clerk perked up, nodding vigorously. Clearly I had said the right thing. Michelangelo, it seemed, was the mayor. We were ushered down a long hallway into a waiting room where a squadron of geezers seemed to be working security. The clerk explained who we were and one of the guys went into the room and soon we were permitted access. It was very *Godfather.* Michelangelo was an Andy Garcia type, young and handsome and wearing a pinstriped suit. We arrived just as he was about to go home for lunch, and he insisted we come with him. On the way out he presented us with a ceramic plaque that was given to all newlyweds in the town. On the back he wrote: *"Comune di Venticano, Prov. di Avellino. A Paolo e Giulia con affetto. A questa nuova famiglia dall'amministrazione comunale gli auguri più belli. Il Sindaco, Dott. Michelangelo Ciarcia 11/10/02."* When we got home my friend Jessica translated it: "The community of Venticano, Avellino province. To Paul and Julie with affection. Best wishes to this new family from the town administration. The Mayor, Michelangelo Ciarcia, October 11, 2002."

. . .

MICHELANGELO was Paul's second cousin, his father was Jean's cousin, and his grandfather was Paul's grandfather's brother.

After meeting Michelangelo's parents and wife and children and eating their lunch (his mother claimed that although she'd made this feast, she wanted only a fried egg), we were taken on a tour of the heart-stoppingly charming town and its various establishments: Vincenzo's prosciutto factory, Niccolo's torrone shop (torrone is kind of like nougat), Vittorio's bakery, packed with biscotti and cookies filled with chocolates and candied fruits. We had our picture taken in front of the church where Paul's grandparents, Nanny Arci and Pop Pop, had been married. Dozens more relatives (most named Giuseppina) embraced and fed us and showed us their photos. One of the Giuseppinas brought Paul almost to tears because she reminded him exactly of his aunt Josephine, who'd died two years before I met him. We sat at her kitchen table, in a kitchen that could've been Jean's kitchen, and talked to her. Though she spoke only Italian and we spoke none, I understood her perfectly. I can't quite explain this, but it was almost the tone of her voice or her heart that spoke.

I remembered something my grandfather wrote in his memoir.

> In 1914, we moved back to the Bronx. During the summer months, all the elderly people would bring out

> chairs and sit across the street in the park and spend the light hours telling each other their problems. As I mentioned earlier, my Bubbe spoke no English, but as most of the neighbors were also Jewish, that presented no problem. However Bubbe seemed to have become particularly friendly with another lady who spoke no English either. She only spoke Italian. Surprisingly, this did not prevent them from sitting together and gossiping all day long.

At the end of the day, we left. The sun finally came out to set and there was a double rainbow in the sky. It was *magnifico*! Paul was snapping pictures of every building, tree, person, and flower as we drove off, a missing piece returned to him.

Flying back to New York, I was never so happy to be going home, except maybe when I returned from the Grand Canyon. We made our impossible connection and I cried. At no point did Paul bring up the word "divorce." We got home late and looked at some mail and went straight to bed. And then a few hours later I woke up. I heard a thud. Paul wasn't in bed, and I jumped up and found him passed out on the bathroom floor. Not home twelve hours and we were back in the hospital.

Apparently the ungodly quantity of savory and sweet carbohydrates Paul had consumed in Italy were not the thing the diabetes doctor had ordered. He stayed in the emergency room, where they stabilized his blood sugar and rehydrated him. I sat on the floor in the hall, thinking about the health of my husband, and the health of our finances. Neither of them was very pleasant to look at. When Paul was feeling better, I'd tell him that he had better get a job soon or else! I would try to get a job, too, but I hadn't been having very much luck on that front. And since I'd never been a very good earner, let's be honest, no one was expecting much from me.

When Paul felt better, we went home. A day later my mother drove Otto back from her house. Our family was together again.

I heard Paul on the phone saying how I kept telling people that Italy sucked. I didn't say Italy sucked, I said our trip sucked. When he got off the phone, we talked.

"It was hard, but I had a wonderful time," I said. I really had a better time than I was letting on; I don't know why I had the need to complain to everyone. I kind of have a policy of always telling people anytime I've traveled that it wasn't good. It stems from the fact that I always feel a wee sense of betrayal when people have had fun without me. When I ask, "How was your trip?" I like to hear, "It was okay," or "So-so," or "Not great." Then I say, "Oh, I'm sorry. Why?" Then they can say, "The food was inedible," or "It rained every day," or "My in-laws are a pain in the ass," or "Our room smelled like cat pee." When people say, "Oh, we had the best time!" I feel kind of sad and left out, so I try not to make others feel that way.

During the summer, before my laser surgery, I'd gone to a doctor for a tranquilizer. In the course of the discussion it came up that after we got married, we wanted to get pregnant. The doctor checked my blood and found that my childhood immunizations had worn off, so I got a booster shot, along with a warning not to get pregnant for six months.

After the time was up, and while we looked for work, we started "trying." Jancee said not to tell people you're trying to have a baby because then they picture you having sex; rather, you should tell them you're planning on having a baby, and that way they imagine you studying your appointment calendar.

I started the process not by putting on a sexy negligee and thigh-high boots, but by navigating through thousands of websites aimed at making you wonder how anyone was born in the world before the Internet. There were so many tips, support chat rooms, and products available, and online calculators that ask you to put in the first day of your last period and then determine the days you'd likely ovulate, the day you would likely conceive, and finally, your due date. There were recommendations to buy an Ovulation Predictor Kit, something you peed on in the morning that told you when you were ovulating and, by extension, when would be the best time to have sex. This was before you peed on something that told you you were or weren't pregnant. The same people who figured out how to make a bundle on brides-to-be had moved on to mothers-to-be. It didn't occur to me that the time I'd been pregnant previously, it had happened while practicing the very methods we used to avoid getting pregnant. From what I recalled, at no time after sex had I ever pushed a pillow under my butt and shot my legs in the air. But you can bet I was going to do it now!

The first month I was so sure I was pregnant that a few days after we "tried" (if you're picturing me having sex, quit it—I assure you it was nothing like what you're imagining), I started taking tests. There are really good early-pregnancy tests, but, as I found, you actually have to be pregnant for them to be able to tell you if you are. There are also sites (I think there was one called amIpregnant.com) that give you the signs and symptoms of pregnancy, which are, remarkably, the very same signs and symptoms you get when you're expecting your period. As a scientific experiment, I quizzed Matt on the signs of pregnancy.

"Do you have stinky pee?" I queried.

"Isn't all pee stinky?" he said.

Touché! Other than sore boobs, which you actually do get if you keep checking them for soreness, he pretty definitely had a bun in the oven.

A hundred bucks later, I was still not pregnant. I was so distraught that I bought the Ovulation Predictor Kit for twenty-five bucks and started Googling "fertility problems." This is why the Internet is bad. Because if you put in that your age is thirty-five, you will be redirected to the geriatric lost-cause sites.

The following month I screwed the whole thing up miserably. With the ovulation kit, you have to pee on the thing just so much and no more or something goes terribly wrong. I peed on it too much, then too little, and then I had the wrong pee of the day. If I couldn't manage to handle this apparatus, how on earth would I be able to be someone's mother? Paul convinced me to "try" anyway, because the kit wasn't directly connected to my reproductive system. I humored him, knowing full well that it was futile, and went about my business of not finding a job.

This is the way my brain operated: I'm not pregnant, could not be, but hopefully will be soon. And then, what if I have a job and I'm pregnant? And then, will my employer get mad if I don't tell him that I'm not pregnant but am planning to become pregnant? Can you see how this line of thinking might get in the way of, say, doing just about anything?

I spoke to Margot extensively, and her comment was, "Pregnant people do work." I knew that because Margot had worked through her pregnancies, right up to the morning when someone, her husband perhaps, called me and said, "Margot is not going to be able to make your appointment this morning because she's had her baby."

For me it was different, since I didn't have a job in place. Nor had I been able to find one when I wasn't trying to get pregnant. Then it was the wedding planning, now it was the pregnancy planning. See, I did have jobs in my mind, like breaking in those shoes; they just didn't happen to pay—and, more likely, they actually cost me.

Jancee and I were on the phone one night talking about our professional frustrations—her unfulfilling, high-paying, high-profile jobs, and my absence of even a paper route. Jancee brought up how well we worked together, and said that perhaps we could work on some big project. We had just cowritten an article for *O,* the Oprah magazine, that went very smoothly. We got loads of appreciative reader mail, and the article was selected to go in a compilation book of the best pieces from the magazine's first five years. We decided to work on coming up with something, and that would at least satisfy the feeling that I wasn't doing anything else.

In the back of my mind, I had a vague awareness that my period was due and there was no sign of it. I checked the sites and I had none of the symptoms, so I went out and bought an enormous box of sanitary pads and waited.

Paul said, "I think you're pregnant."

"I'm not pregnant. My period is always erratic. Don't set yourself up for disappointment."

Just to be sure, I took a test. It was negative.

"See?" I said. "I knew it. I know my body."

A few days later my period still hadn't arrived, so I started wearing pads because I just knew it was coming any minute and it would be heavy. Another day, and another, and I bought another test. Negative was one pink line, positive two lines. I peed on the thing, and there appeared very faint lines—two of them.

I was having a very faint baby. Maybe it would be simply vapor; perhaps it would join the Super Friends, able to seep under doorways and through keyholes like Green Lantern. Vaporino or Vaporina, depending on the sex. I didn't tell anyone, which was shocking because I told everyone everything that happened to me. The test said whether the lines were dark or light, you were pregnant, but we decided to do another test the next morning. I half expected that the lines would have faded away. But they hadn't. The two lines were dark, distinct, pink. I was going to have a human baby. I went to the online calculator and determined my due date: September 28, 2003.

When I told people that I was pregnant, the most common response was, "Wow, that was fast!"

I was surprised that I was pregnant because of the statistics I had read: almost fifty percent of couples take more than six months to get pregnant, while some take over a year and a half. But it was no less than I expected from my body. Though I had a complete lack of confidence in myself professionally, I had total faith in my body. There were those things my mother always told me about "us," her and me. We were not hairy, and we were very fertile.

"So much better than being hirsute and barren," Barbara would say. Her mother told her things about the girls in her family, too—that they had no upper-arm strength.

According to our mothers, Barbara would be lucky if she could lift a glass to her lips, while I would multiply like Mrs. Peter Rabbit and never have to worry about mustache bleach.

It occurred to me that my mother had gotten married at twenty-two and had my brothers and me at twenty-four, twenty-six, and twenty-eight, respectively, and I was now thirty-five (almost thirty-six). Still, she had been right, because I was pregnant. I also assumed I'd have the same kind of pregnancy as she did. Easy. Pregnancy agreed with her. In the 8 mm film of baby me on Mom's lap the Memorial Day after I was born (which would've made me seven months old at the time), she was wearing a string bikini and there was no fat in sight.

That became my postpregnancy image: I'd be wearing a

bikini (though I never had worn one before I was pregnant) and I'd have a toe-tappin', finger-snappin' pregnancy, and then I'd be a tight little new mom. During the nine months I'd look like Demi Moore on the cover of *Vanity Fair*, and at the end I'd pop out my baby like a champagne cork. Then, when the first baby was ten months old, I'd get pregnant with number two. And then we'd see from there.

I had no signs of pregnancy until about nine weeks, then I felt a teeny bit sick, then I felt disgusting. I had heard the nausea lasted until anywhere from twelve to sixteen weeks. I could live with that, I figured. A few days after I discovered I was pregnant, Paul got a call about a supervising producer job at a show on VH1. The pay was good and he was exactly what they were looking for. Within a few weeks he started his job and we were back on solid footing. The only negative about the job was that Paul's boss was the biggest jackass on the planet. He'd leave messages for Paul on our home answering machine on a Saturday morning, yelling about one thing or another. I don't know if it was hormones or what, but I had this long-running daily fantasy about killing the guy with karate. I don't know karate, but in my mind this guy did end up in a bloody heap.

Still, I felt like things were as they should be: Paul was making money, I was making a baby. Pregnancy saved me from once again addressing the fact that I couldn't manage to do anything financially productive.

My big-picture plan was that after "the kids" were off to school, I'd do something like work in an art gallery. Jancee and I had started writing a script together, a romantic comedy. Since she was in Brooklyn and I was on the Upper West Side, we'd do it over the phone. During an initial planning meeting over tea sandwiches and pink cakes at the Pierpont Morgan Library, we scanned the wall of benefactors' names to choose our characters—we thought it would make a great story when we were interviewed on the talk-show circuit. Very soon after our first meeting, I began to experience the unearthly first-trimester exhaustion. When I read that Sarah Jessica Parker had halted shooting on *Sex and the City* during her first trimester because she was just too tired, I felt much better. Jancee, however, wanted to get some work done. She called me in the morning.

"Did you have coffee?" she'd ask.

"No, I can't drink coffee," I'd say.

"Oh," Jancee bubbled up, "feeling pretty good?"

"No," I said. I wanted to get fired.

"Do you not want to do this?"

"I don't, but let's do it anyway."

I sat down at my computer and we got to work, in theory. Jancee was Señorita Firecracker and I was Sidewalk Gum. I'd start formatting the pages, we'd write a scene setup, and then I'd need a nap. From the other end of the line, Jancee tried to bolster me, like walking around a drunken college kid at a frat party.

"You can do it! Focus!"

Prepregnancy, I was known to write twenty pages a day; here I was doing one and a half, with help. At the end of every session, Jancee begged me to call her again when my energy was back up. I felt like the Cowardly Lion in the field of poppies. Finally I gave in and spent my days in bed with Otto, reading novels.

Paul and I had both noticed a change in Otto since we'd come back from our honeymoon. He'd stare into space for long periods of time and didn't want to get on the bed. There was a certain amount of joie de vivre missing, and the graying of his muzzle made me think it was just age.

One morning, he didn't seem well and, ignoring my now pregnant stomach, I carried his twenty-four-pound body several blocks to the vet.

I had phoned Paul at work; we thought maybe he'd ingested pesticide in the park. The vet wanted me to leave him so they could monitor him and give him charcoal to make him throw up and an IV so he wouldn't get dehydrated. When Otto didn't seem to care that I was leaving I got really worried. They told me to call at five, but at four I went over there to wait with Mattie.

The vet came out and said Otto was fine, and then they opened the door to the kennel. Now, no dog with half a brain likes the vet, and recently Otto's abhorrence had reached new levels. He'd shake insanely, gasp for air, and stretch his leash to press his face against the door to leave the minute we came in.

When the tech brought him out to me that day, he didn't jump up on me or dance or wag his tail. He just approached me, barely acknowledging my presence. As we were leaving, the vet said to me, "He does have some kind of heart arrhythmia, but not bad." He walked over to his desk and said, "He's a healthy dog and he's going to live a good long time." Then he knocked wood.

He wasn't fine. In fact, in the back of my mind I remember wondering how the vet could let him go in that condition, but I was just glad to bring him home.

Mattie dropped us off at the park near our apartment so he could walk a bit before going in. He just stood there. He wouldn't pee. Another dog came by and he didn't move. We went into the building and he walked slowly; the heavy, old elevator door closed on the middle of his body, and I forced it open, screaming and cursing about "this fucking building's fucking elevator." An Orthodox woman stared at me like I was insane.

Inside, I made him some chicken and rice, which he didn't smell or touch. I called Paul and asked him to come home, then canceled an appointment I had with Margot. Otto was just way too uncomfortable to be left alone.

Paul called the vet when he got home and they suggested placing a heating pad on our laps with a towel over it and him on top. It didn't work. Somehow he fell asleep at 10:30. We both lay on the floor beside him, petting him and kissing him until we fell asleep. An hour later I woke up and Otto was standing in the middle of the room gasping for air. I woke Paul and said we should take him to the Animal Medical Center.

By the time we got dressed, he was lying on the floor, no longer in control of his bodily functions. I wrapped him up in a fleece blanket and Paul carried him while I raced to find a cab. Sometime during that endless ride, he got very still and his eyes glazed over.

"Is he dead?" I said urgently to Paul.

"I don't know."

I decided he must be in shock. We took him to the emergency room and said, "We have a very sick doggy here." We were swiftly ushered into an examining room. A young attending vet came in and looked at Otto, placing his stethoscope on Otto's heart.

"I'm sorry."

We stayed with him in the room for an hour; the kind young vet made an imprint of his paw in clay for us to bake and keep. I felt like my insides were on the floor beneath me. The pain was as bottomless as our love for him. We walked out sobbing, and I called Mattie, who lived two blocks away.

"Otto's gone," I sobbed.

"Where did he go?" she said.

It was two in the morning, and she walked to meet us with tears streaming down her face. Otto adored Mattie; she had driven me to pick him up from the rescuer in Pennsylvania in 1996.

Mattie and my uncle Dave and Paul and I sat up till close to five a.m., telling Otto stories and crying. We were indeed sitting shiva.

The only day worse than that day was the next day, waking up to no Otto, and all that that entailed. The subsequent encompassing grief was like nothing I'd ever experienced. It took two weeks before I could actually put on any mascara, another week after that until it stopped streaming down my face sometime during the day.

There was a biography special on Edgar Allan Poe on cable that Saturday night. They began listing the tragedies of his life, how all of his "dearest" family died before their time. I kept thinking when they said, "His dear mother died," "His dear wife died," that if they said, "And then his dear dog died," people would think it was a joke.

Every action in my life involved Otto. My putting on shoes, if he was going out with me, evoked a joyous dance. If he wasn't going I would resolutely not make eye contact with him. Leftover food suddenly seemed pointless. Joy seemed pointless. And unfair. The moon went out. For a month our house was filled with flowers and condolence cards, and a friend made a donation to a large animal shelter in Otto's name. There was never a more fitting tribute; Otto was simply the best example of a pound dog around.

In the end it was his heart that failed; the right diagnosis was missed. It made sense to me that he had died of an enlarged heart. He had perhaps the largest heart of any being I knew.

A week to the day after he died, I got a call from my obstetrician. She was reviewing one of my pregnancy tests, something called AFP. Though it was only a screening, the results were worrisome: according to the test, I had a one-in-thirteen chance of carrying a baby with Down syndrome. We had planned to have an amniocentesis the following week, but she wanted us to hurry it up, go today, just in case.

I felt such a raw terror, I went numb. When we got to the hospital, the genetic counselor told us we should probably not ask about the sex of the baby till the results came back, just in case. I guess she figured we wouldn't be bonded to this baby if we only knew it was either a boy or a girl.

Soon after we went into the examining room, a doctor I hadn't met before came in. He was so steady and normal and self-assured. After looking at my test results, his confidence was shaken momentarily. A sonogram was set up and he looked at the picture of the baby.

"I'm not doing an amnio," he said. "It's too early. There's nothing wrong with this baby, and if we do it too early we could cause a miscarriage."

I didn't speak. I had sonogram goo on my belly; let someone else talk.

"So you think it's okay," Paul said.

"If I were in Vegas," he said, looking us both in the eyes, "I would bet it all that this baby is fine."

He explained that there are "soft indicators," things you can see on a sonogram. None of them was there, not to mention the fact that the other tests we had taken all came out well.

As he left the room, telling us to come back in two weeks, he said, "Stop worrying, you're having a baby! It's not a disease!"

We looked at him like two frozen fish.

"You want to know what you're having?" he asked.

When I muttered that the genetics person told us not to ask about the sex, he shook his head in an I'll-deal-with-her-later manner.

"Sure!" Paul said.

It was a wonderful moment, because no matter what that doctor told me, until the test results came back, I was not going to feel relieved. But Paul was confident, and I'd go along with that.

We already knew what we were having, though. Everyone who looked at me said it was a boy. We knew his name: Oliver Roger.

"Sure!" Paul said.

"A girl," he said, looking back at the sonogram. "And from the looks of it, a very tall girl."

"We'll need a different name," I told Paul.

For the two weeks leading to the next amnio and the two weeks waiting for the result, I channeled my crippling fear into *American Idol.* Each week there were two shows: an evening of performances and then the results show. For four weeks, Ruben Studdard stood in for the health of my baby. If Ruben was okay, she would be okay.

At the end of four weeks, Ruben was a winner, and the tests showed that Baby Girl Leo was, too.

Eleven

No Place to Go but the Animal Psychic

THE FIRST KOOKY THING I did after it was all clear was call an animal psychic I had once talked to, to see if Otto was okay in the afterworld. I decided that between grief and hormones and the fact that I couldn't drink alcohol or take tranquilizers or get my hair highlighted, I could talk to whomever the hell I wanted.

She said a lot of things, but the thing that stuck in my head was that Otto had died so he could go over to the "other side" and help me with the birth of my baby. Everything was going to be okay, she said, but it was going to be a difficult birth.

No, I said to myself, because the bad is over and the baby is fine and that's that.

I'd started to feel better, and soon I had energy enough to do the second kooky thing. Here's a riddle. What is the one thing a couple having their first baby don't need? Answer: a puppy!

Very soon after Otto died, I made Paul call my old vet, a lovely man and a Boston terrier breeder on the Upper West Side, just to tell him what happened and to ask if he knew of anyone who sometime in the future might have Boston terrier puppies. The vet told Paul that at the moment *he* had a pregnant bitch.

Paul replied, "So do I!" while I groaned with forced laughter. He knew she would be having three puppies, and that they were all females. He was going to keep one, he said, give one to his secretary, and for the third one there was a waiting list of about seventy-five people. Within minutes our red checker had jumped over all the other black checkers and we were first in line. We were now expecting two babies.

Hook was the fattest dog in the litter, and when we first came to see her, she hid behind a box and every so often peered around to check to see if we had left yet.

Paul renamed her Beatrice. She was so tiny that our Boston terrier doorstop dwarfed her. A few days after we got her I went to the gym, and when I came home I couldn't find her. I was convinced she had fallen out the tiny crack of window I'd left open. I called Paul and told him to come home, I'd meet him in the lot behind the building to look for her remains.

The doorman and I scoured the area, and then I went

back upstairs to take another look—she was sleeping in the back of her crate. A little stuffed panda had been blocking my view of her.

That night the breeder called to check and see how she was doing.

"What would we have told him if she'd fallen out the window today?" I asked Paul when I'd hung up.

"We'd have told him we wanted our money back," he said. "This dog can't fly."

Other than the fact that I looked like a balloon in the Macy's parade, I was doing okay. I was really concerned with just how fat I was. By the end of my first trimester I had porked up twenty-five pounds. I boasted to everyone how it was really a triumph, that I had achieved what it took most gals nine months to do in a mere three. I was done. I'd gained all of my weight; the rest of the pregnancy I could kick back and relax.

My mother said she "carried large." That was her euphemism. I didn't know this until I was pregnant, but apparently I have a tipped uterus, so, as my OB said, my belly wouldn't "pop out" till much later. I thought perhaps it was tipped back so far that the baby was actually in my ass.

One of the nurses in the office was very critical of me so I changed my "starting weight" on my pregnancy chart the next time I was left alone with a pen in the examining room.

"It's a New York thing!" my mother said about the skinny-pregnancy obsession. I saw women in my neighborhood walking around with new babies wearing their size 2 jeans. Maybe I was carrying one of those *Weekly World News* fifty-pound babies. I could hope. On the elliptical machine at the gym, I watched endless hours of daytime TV makeover shows in which they taught women who never lost their baby weight how to wear drapey clothes to appear more slender. I began to vacillate between fears of being a bad mother and fears of being a fat mother.

One day in the laundry room I innocently asked a woman from my building what school her daughters went to.

"I don't think you should be worrying about schools yet," she said, frowning at me.

"I'm worried about everything," I admitted.

There was the money issue: Paul's job was on a show that would be ending right about the time the baby was born. I worried about space: our one-bedroom, which had once felt palatial, now resembled a pet-store birdcage. I worried about mean kids, learning disabilities, being a competent parent, sleep deprivation, nursing, losing weight, getting to the gym, how I was going to walk the dog while pushing the baby carriage, Paul's health, if I was ever going to feel well, hormones, my back pain getting so bad I wouldn't be able to lift my baby, and going completely insane.

Paul was worried that the music in my iPod would go through my head, down my throat, and into the baby's ears, that the first album she'd be exposed to would be *Power Hits of the '80s*, that she'd be born singing "Come On, Eileen."

Cheryl was extremely comforting. Her one bit of advice was not to read about the complications in the back of every pregnancy book. Fair enough. I talked a lot about being fat. Matt said I didn't look fat, my head just looked really, really tiny.

On a particularly hot summer day, around thirty weeks, I started to feel strange. I'd gone to get my hair cut and the stylist was trying to make my hair big to downplay my body. When I left the salon, I realized that I was not feeling the baby move, so I called my OB, crying, and was told to go to the hospital. On the way there, I felt a small kick, or gas, I didn't know which. By the time I checked in to triage, the baby was doing the hustle and I thanked the woman at the desk and prepared to go.

"You can't leave until you get checked out," she said. I guess it was a malpractice thing. I ended up being there for seven hours. The baby was moving, but my blood pressure, normally low, was so high I thought the machine was broken. I went to three different beds and monitors before finally conceding it was me. I was also having some small contractions, which appeared on the monitor—my insides felt like I was going over a bump in a car—and I had a flash of recognition as I realized this was what I'd been feeling all throughout the past week. Who knew? They let me leave finally, but I was ordered to see my doctor first thing the next day.

Again with the blood pressure, and I had gained twenty pounds since my last visit. What the hell? The doctor said it looked like preeclampsia. I was officially on bed rest and needed to do a twenty-four-hour urine screen.

She gave me a giant bottle that said URINE on it and a discreet bag that I could carry it in that said **URINE**. She told me to collect all of my pee for twenty-four hours, bring it back the next day, and we'd go from there. I looked at the little spout and wondered how in the hell I would be able to make that happen. My biggest concern was that I was going to pee on my hand.

I stood on Central Park West for forty minutes waiting for a taxi, and I cried the whole way home because I felt like it. When I got home, I looked up preeclampsia online and found that it's a hypertensive disorder of pregnancy that could come just before delivery but that usually rears its ugly head after twenty weeks. It's characterized by high blood pressure and protein in the urine. Some of the symptoms include swelling, rapid weight gain, headaches, and changes in vision, or there could be no symptoms. Hypertensive disorders of pregnancy are the leading worldwide cause of maternal and infant illness and death.

The conservative guess is that it causes 76,000 deaths each year.

Maternal and infant deaths. Deaths? DEATHS? I called Paul and my mother and Mattie and Matt and Cheryl. Mattie came over; Paul was on his way.

Mattie arrived with a bag of presents: glitter, crayons, a pad, glue, markers, and some magazines, including one called *Hairdo Ideas*. She hugged me a lot and said everything would be fine.

We were lying in my bed, watching *To Sir, with Love*, eating candy, and talking about what we'd do when the baby came, to punish it for scaring me. Mattie kept saying she wanted to give the baby gum.

Just when I thought it would be okay, the electricity went

off. We figured we had used too much air-conditioning and checked the circuit breakers. They were fine, but oddly the lights in the hall were off, too, and then we heard people shouting.

Mattie, who was in New York during the Great Blackout of 1977, gave me a weak smile. She knew right away.

As luck would have it, my preeclampsia struck at the same moment as the Great Blackout of 2003. We couldn't get through to anyone because all of our phones were cordless and wireless. It got hotter and hotter and more chaotic. Mattie wouldn't leave, and Paul had to walk home from work, which entailed climbing down forty-five flights of stairs, walking sixty-plus blocks, and then climbing the seven flights of stairs to our apartment. It took a while, but he arrived with a plug-in phone and a transistor radio and water. By five in the morning, our power was restored. All through the night I'd been having contractions and peeing into my bottle by candlelight, and I was no frontier woman.

The next day, after the preeclampsia was confirmed, my mother arrived. I had to make regular visits to the hospital to monitor the baby and my urine. Lights or no lights, it was a bitch getting that pee in that bottle. Fortunately, I was peeing so much, I had urine to spare. I cried every day, twice a day. My mom stayed for the whole week and came back the following Monday.

Margot was in Europe through Labor Day, so I left her a message about what was going on. She called me back.

"Just don't ask me how I'm holding up, because I'm not," I told her.

"Maybe it's not a bad thing to have bed rest."

"I have so much to do!" I complained. "I'm not ready!"

"No one's ever ready. You could be pregnant for years and you still wouldn't be ready."

"But I have to get my nursing bra and the bassinet sheets and the storage bags for the breast milk and"—I was crying again, this time on international-long-distance rates.

"Just try and relax, okay?" she said soothingly. "And leave me a message on my machine if you want to talk again."

When I hung up with her I felt better; she was so calm and reassuring, and she knew me so well. I'd been her patient going on twenty years, and there was a level of intimacy impossible to explain.

When I'd gotten the positive results of the amnio, I decided to make a picture (mixed media) for my baby girl. Paul bought me a huge canvas and paints and glitter and crayons. I drew a mermaid and a bunch of sea creatures and then I stuck the canvas behind the couch. When I was bedbound, I dug it out and resumed working on it. I was Frida Kahlo without the talent. I'd send Paul e-mails to go to trimming shops in the Thirty-fourth Street area for certain items I needed for my "piece." My mother brought some shocking-pink sequins she'd found in her sewing box for the mermaid's bikini top. Three weeks into the preeclampsia, I finished the picture. The very last part was a soft-green diamond-shaped piece of sea glass that I'd found in Barbados. It became the jewel in the mermaid's crown.

At night my mother went to sleep at Mattie's—she

wanted to give Paul and me space. She was so wonderful that I couldn't imagine how I'd ever function without her and I hoped my daughter would love me one-tenth as much as I loved her.

I was at thirty-three weeks, and we were all so happy I hadn't had to give birth yet that we thought I might actually make it to my shower. It was Wednesday and the shower was Saturday. I squished myself into the dress I planned to wear and thought maybe it would be better to skip it. How was it going to work? I'd lie on my couch? It was all a little too pathetic. No matter, though, because at nine p.m. my doctor's office called and said the recent urine was lousy with protein and I should go to the hospital, bring my bag, and plan to stay.

I took a shower because I thought it would be good to meet my new daughter with clean hair. I hadn't had my pedicure done as the books suggested. It lost its urgency under the circumstances.

We arrived at the hospital. They checked my blood pressure, and it was sky-high. I was admitted, and they decided to put an end to my preeclampsia with the only cure known: delivery.

The plan was to induce, but I wasn't dilated at all, so—okay, stop. I am not going to replay the labor story. You know it was long and bad. The only thing I will say is, I need not have washed my hair, as it was continually vomited on. What seemed like twenty years later, but was actually the next day at 4:50 p.m., neither the baby nor I was doing too hot, and they couldn't afford to wait any longer so they did a C-section. Paul, who'd had to change into scrubs, sat beside me behind the curtain. Here's what I heard.

Doctor to resident: "Okay, you have to pull her out fast, time is of the essence. Forget it, I'll do it!"

Doctor to room: "Here she is—OOOH, *she's scrawny!*"

Scrawny? The last sonogram had her at nearly six pounds—not *Weekly World News*–worthy, but not that bad.

Nurse's voice: "Four pounds, four ounces."

Doctor: "Take her to the NICU"—the neonatal intensive care unit.

Someone asked what her name was.

"Violet Jean Leo," I said as I watched the brief flash of purple wet baby go by. I didn't see her again for twenty-four hours, because I was in recovery and she was in the NICU and neither of us was supposed to move.

I finally lost it; I had to see my baby. They had given me a Polaroid of her, but that just wasn't enough. I was wheeled in my bed into the NICU so I could see her and hold her.

She was in an incubator, skinny but long with several wires hooked up to her wrist and ankle and a little heart-shaped monitor on her chest. Over her eyes were pads; she was jaundiced and under the lights. They pushed me up beside her box and the nurse told me to speak to her.

"Hello, my sweet baby girl. Hi, my love," I said, and her little head perked up. She recognized the sound of my voice. They took her out for a very short time so I could hold her. She was warm and tan from the lights and her hair was blond. She was so small there was nothing I could compare her to. She weighed less than the chicken I'd baked for dinner a few nights before.

We found out that sonograms are not terribly accurate, and that she probably hadn't been getting enough nutrients for the past week. It was the first of many "please kill me now" moments. So although she'd grown in length, her tummy was concave. Oy. Oy. Oy.

While I lay in the hospital bed eating ice chips, Mattie called and asked if I wanted her to bring me some of the hors d'oeuvres she had made for my shower (a clam dip, some brie en croute, assorted crackers). You know, in case the people coming to see the baby wanted something to nosh on. I told her I would not, under any circumstances, be putting out a spread in my hospital room.

In a few days I was mobile and going for feedings, and a few days after that I was discharged, but Violet remained in the hospital. It's not a good feeling to come home from the hospital without a baby after having one. Paul and I visited her in the mornings, then he went to work and came back at lunch and again in the evening. I sat by her isolette all day long, boring her into recovery. I sang songs to her, like the theme from the movie *Arthur*—"*When you get caught between the moon and New York City . . . the best that you can do is fall in love.*" Or *Tootsie*—"*Wishin' there would be someone waiting home for me . . . Something's telling me it might be you all of my life.*"

I told her that when we sprang her from this joint, we were going to Saks for lunch, where Bubbe (my mother), Mattie, and I would have the chicken mandarin salad and she'd have milk. I questioned her about the "other side" and asked if she'd met a small black-and-white gentleman who went by the name Otto. I asked her about this thing I heard, that babies are supposed to bring money. I mean, she didn't even carry a wallet. I told her that she could be whatever she wanted to be, but not to listen to everyone who was telling her that with her long fingers she should be a pianist—whoever heard of a newborn playing the piano, anyway?

Margot came and visited. We actually had a session in the New Parents' Lounge (but I didn't lie down). After it was over she asked to see Violet and I brought her back. She cried and hugged me and said, "Oh, Julie! She's beautiful." She sniffed, "I feel like a grandmother!"

She gushed, "I'm so happy. Except for being very thin, she looks really fine." It's true, she wasn't one of those fit-in-your-hand preemies.

"She's like you, Julie," Margot said, hugging me again. "There's nothing wrong with her, she just needs to grow."

Soon after her postbirth weight loss, she bulked up to a hefty four pounds, eight ounces. Finally, we could take her home. Until that time, I didn't feel like she was really mine. It was like she had been the property of the nurses and the hospital.

And then she was Mine. No more cords and pads on her eyes. She grew at an astounding rate. All she did was eat, night and day, God bless her. At birth she was below the charts, but that was soon going to change.

Violet continued to thrive, but we didn't. Paul's job ended, and there was nothing on the horizon. We were frighteningly low on funds, so we borrowed money from my father. It ran out and things were still going south, so Paul asked Jean if she could lend us some. She said no. She didn't explain at the time, but it turned out she had been in the midst of a complicated transfer of funds involving trusts and taxes and it just wasn't available. I mistook it for tough love. She was not sympathetic, and was a little angry about Paul's difficulty finding a job. In her experience, if you needed a job, you just *got* a job. I knew how different she was from my mother. They both loved their children, but Jean didn't coddle, while my mother seemed anxious to take a bullet for me at every turn. Who's to say which way is better? I did start to understand that there are different ways to love your children. I also understood that you can parent two kids in the exact same way, and one turns out to be Bill Clinton and the other to be Roger Clinton. It isn't an exact science.

For Thanksgiving the whole Leo family convened at Jean's home. The first thing I noticed was how terrible Jean looked and how down she seemed. Something wasn't right. A week or so afterward she told us she'd been having trouble walking and was coming back into Manhattan for some scans. The cancer had come back and spread. I met Paul and Bob and Debbye at the hospital. Paul was alone with Jean in her room, and when I came in they were both crying.

Bob and Debbye came in, followed by the doctor, who wanted to discuss whether Jean would be more comfortable at home or in hospice. I bit my lips and cheeks to keep from crying—that wasn't going to help anyone. Of all people, Jean noticed and squeezed my hand. She told the doctor she'd like to stay at Bob's, that she was comfortable there and would not like to go into hospice. It was December 19 and we had all been discussing Christmas plans. We figured Jean would be there through Christmas and we'd reevaluate where she'd stay after New Year's. The next day, a Saturday, Paul went down to see her at Bob's, and he said she was sleeping. Monday, Violet and I went with him and found her virtually in a coma. We brought a screaming Violet to her bedside, and Jean's eyes opened for a second and she said, "Shhhh, shhhhh."

The next day she was worse, and they decided to move her to a hospice facility nearby. You could tell she was in pain, even though she wasn't talking or fully awake. Paul and Bob went with her in the ambulance and spent the next two nights sleeping on the floor at the hospice. The next day was Christmas Eve, and Paul's brother John and his family came in. John and Paul visited most of the day. Paul and I decided we'd spend Christmas Day with her.

Down the hall from the room Jean shared with another woman, there was a family room. It was a place to get away from the gloom of the patients' rooms. Volunteers had put up a tree and decorated it and made a big turkey dinner. They came to Jean's room and invited us to the meal. It was an incredibly moving thing to meet these people who had volunteered to spend Christmas Day with the families of people who were dying. I sat in the hall, feeding Violet, and one of the volunteers, a man in his fifties, asked me if I needed anything.

"It is so extraordinarily kind of you to be here today of all days," I said.

"It's much easier for me to be here than you," he said. "Of that I am sure."

He patted my hand and walked on.

Late in the day, Bob called and asked us to come to his house. We should all eat sandwiches together and then go back later.

We opened some gifts. Jean had given Debbye, an amazing craftswoman, some keepsakes of hers to put in a shadow box for Violet. Surrounding a picture of Jean as a beautiful little girl were her baby bonnet and baby necklace and some charms. Debbye had also made copies of pictures of Jean for everyone.

At a few minutes to six, we got our coats. Violet was asleep and we needed to get her home. As we stood at the door saying our good-byes, the phone must have rung. A moment later Bob came over and told us that at six p.m. Jean had passed away.

Twelve

Finding My Inner Erin Brockovich

By hook or by crook, I was growing up. Paul continued looking for work and writing a script. Violet was growing beautifully, regardless of her little Phil Collins peninsula of hair.

A year later, we moved to a two-bedroom apartment six blocks north, on Broadway. The rent was a few hundred dollars more than we were paying, but electricity was included and we could install a washer and dryer.

It was a charming place, a grand old prewar doorman building, with a great staff: they were funny, nice, and always up for talking Mets and Yankees with Paul. Most important, the rental office accepted us even though our income was zero.

After looking at apartments for even a brief time in Manhattan you learn one thing: if it sounds too good to be true, it is. There is a way of spinning everything; a hole in the floor is a place for an indoor swimming pool. And God help you if they're looking for do-it-yourselfers. You'll be lucky to *have* a floor. Once Paul went to look at an apartment in Hudson Heights, along the Hudson River above Harlem. It was advertised as having "the most amazing river views I've ever seen." When Paul arrived, the broker showed him the river views. Outside and to the left of the building. From inside the apartment, you got a view of a brick wall that needed pointing.

A friend of my father's in Vermont was assessed an extra tax for his mountain views (what if you're blind or, like me, you hate mountains?). I'm not sure who we have to thank, but we seem to be the only people in the city who aren't charged for what we can see out our windows.

Among the extraordinary vistas from our sixteenth-floor windows are unobstructed city views; we can see all the way across the East River to no fewer than eight bridges and Queens. To the north we see the Cathedral of St. John the Divine, the spires of Riverside Church, and the dome of the Low Library at Columbia University, and if I hang out the window and look south I can see the hotels along Central Park South and the Citicorp and GE buildings in midtown and some other building that is topped with a vast lit-up sphere.

We can also see something that people in rural areas take for granted: the sky. On clear nights I sit at my bedroom window with my Peterson's *Field Guide to Stars and Planets*, picking out the individual stars that make up the sword that hangs from Orion's belt.

When we first moved in, those views maintained my sanity. Watching the planes take off from La Guardia, my head hanging out the window, I'd say, "One day we'll be on one of those planes to Hollywood for meetings with producers who want to make our movies for millions!"

And Paul would say, "What? I can't hear you when your head is out the window."

You never think of planes as going to a funeral in Ithaca or an orthodontists' convention in Omaha. Planes have to be going somewhere good—to Rio to sunbathe and sail on Simon Le Bon's yacht with the rest of Duran Duran.

Home, though, increasingly became someplace not so good. Work and Paul weren't finding each other, and I developed some eyebrow furrows you could kayak through.

Much sooner than expected, we went through our savings and Paul's bequest from his mother. There was little money being earned and way way way too much money being borrowed. After an extremely promising interview and follow-up, our prayers seemed to be answered. Paul was up for a job at *Sesame Street*. Not only could he make a decent salary, and benefits, but it would be fun and creative and Violet could meet Elmo. In a ruthlessly crushing blow, someone else got the job. What a strange thing to hear yourself say "Fuck *Sesame Street*!"

This was new territory, the Dakotas of the financially damned. My credit cards didn't work, my ATM card was useless, and I was so depressed and anxious I felt like I might have a breakdown. I needed tranquilizers to fall asleep every night. Margot and I talked on the phone.

"I look horrible," I told her. She hadn't seen me in a while because I had a hard time getting out of the house without Violet.

Margot waited for me to go on.

"I haven't had my hair cut or colored in a year. I'm breaking out like I just hit puberty, and my size zero jeans are so big I look like Jared from the Subway commercials!"

Margot's early training had been in eating disorders. We had been talking about this, and she had recently sent me to a doctor to determine if I was in danger. I wasn't officially underweight, just on the low end of normal; in other words, I looked like every other woman in the city.

Margot felt that my thinning was a silent protest to the money stresses and Paul's health problems. I thought it was funny that I should be accused of doing anything "silent."

"You need to work," she said.

"I can't leave Violet," I said, tears burning my eyes. "And what job could I get? Go back to insurance? It would kill me to leave her."

One friend I was close to who was a working mom said her entire salary went to child care. I didn't see that I could do any better. That kind of situation wasn't going to help us.

Silence.

"I need to be able to go out to lunch and get my hair done and go into Barneys and buy five hundred dollars' worth of makeup."

"I don't buy that," Margot said.

"I do!"

"Julie, lunches and hair appointments are not going to solve your problems."

"But if I could afford them, that would mean my problems were solved."

"I don't think so," she said very emphatically.

"I feel like jumping out a window."

She and I had a much more direct way of communicating than we used to.

"You're jumping out of your skin," she said. "I think you are furious, enraged, and you've got to feel more in control. What about the writing?"

I sighed. I hated pitching and being rejected, and it just didn't seem like it would make any difference. When I did get an assignment, which was rare, it took half a year to get paid for it.

I told her about some women I'd overheard talking. One of them was telling the other about her sister-in-law whose husband was out of work; they had just sold their ski house. The other woman, clipped and intolerant, said, "Well, she's going to have to get a job."

The first woman shot back, "She's incapable." End of conversation.

Why was she incapable? Was she taking care of a disabled child at home? Was she a crackhead? Was she like me?

We talked a bit more, and then I hung up the phone and sat on my bed, staring at the planes taking off. A jewelry box Paul had given me on the first Christmas we were together caught my eye. I brought it onto the bed and began picking through it, mechanically. I always had that fantasy of handing my jewelry down to my little girl, but right now we needed to pay our health insurance and our rent and everything else, close to $10,000, and we had no income. There were a lot of gold bracelets, heavy chains from the eighties, lovely small rings with precious and semiprecious stones: a sapphire, a ruby, an emerald, a pearl, an amethyst, all surrounded by tiny diamonds. There was the only piece I ever got from my Grandma Billie, who was herself a jeweler: a gold bird with a diamond-chip eye. I fingered my mother's pearl choker with the pearl heart clasp that belonged to my grandmother, and which my mother wore to her wedding, and I wore to my ninth-grade prom. I slid everything in the box into a small velvet bag, except a diamond and platinum double chain, my Grandma Pearl's, which I slipped around my neck. I found the GIA certificate that came with my engagement ring in the lock box and stuck it in my purse. I had decided to keep my diamond wedding band, my mother's pearl choker, and Grandma Pearl's necklace, unless of course I got an offer I couldn't refuse.

Paul was reading the paper when I told him I decided to sell my ring.

"Don't you like it?" he asked.

I got on a train to midtown and headed to a well-known jewelry buyer on Fifth Avenue. The son of the owner had been in my Lamaze class and was a very nice guy.

I cried the whole way there, feeling so totally sorry for

myself. I called my mother as I walked past Gucci and Prada and Saks.

"I think you're doing the right thing," she said. "They're just *objects.*" This from the woman who gasped at the notion of a wedding band with diamonds that only made it halfway around. *"And what happens when you have to wave good-bye?"* she'd ask. Because there would be no diamonds facing the person you were waving good-bye to, and then they'd collapse, confused and repulsed, wondering, *"WHERE WERE THE REST OF THE DIAMONDS? WHY DID THEY JUST END LIKE THAT?"* And you would forever inhabit the cloak of shame.

On the journey home, I cried more. I had sold all of my gold for $400, but none of my diamonds were worth anywhere near what they were insured for. The guy generously offered me a third of the amount for my ring, but I declined. My grandmother's diamond platinum necklace was the big-ticket item. I couldn't sell it, though; it was too important to me. Later my mother told me that the necklace had once belonged to William Holden's wife.

I left with my check, $400, enough to cover one minimum payment on one credit card.

How did this happen to me? Was no one looking out for me? Did none of the people who died watch over me from above? Were Grandma Pearl and Grandpa Saul playing gin? I was going to sell my diamonds, for chrissakes.

These were some grim days. I took Violet to a play group because it was free, unlike the $500 forty-five-minute music and gym classes. I felt guilty about not enrolling Violet with the rest of the Upper West Side kids, but Margot made me feel better. She said you spend half the time dressing and undressing them and then they end up wandering away from the circle anyway. The mothers in my play group were smart and sane, if not quite as miserable as me. Every so often others would drift into the fray and I'd fixate on how out of touch they were with anything resembling my life. For one thing, they had no money problems.

I was at one such gathering when two visitors were sitting and talking about the hilarity of getting their babies passport photos. One, a brunette with a hairband/ponytail combo, had been to Provence. Two, a blonde with a Martha Stewart haircut and no roots, had been to London with her husband, who I think she said was a "money buyer." One was on the floor, absorbed by her roly-poly seven-month-old son when he toppled over.

"Oops!" she said, righting him.

Two, who had a five-month-old, studied One carefully and said, "Oh, you say 'oops' when he falls?"

One answered confidently, "Sometimes I say 'oops' or 'oopsie,' or even 'whoopsie.'"

Two took it in, nodding, committing this diamond of mothering advice to memory. I wondered whether, if I banged their two heads together, One would say "ouch" or "ow" or "owie."

Mostly I preferred being on my own. Violet and I spent endless hours on the couch watching preschool television (anything but *Sesame Street*). I thought far too much about the characters on the shows I watched, wondering where Max and Ruby's parents were and why Arthur the aardvark had a pet dog, when all of his friends were animals. I wondered if other people got hungry when they watched *Miffy*, a show where everyone looked like a cookie or a brownie to me.

I considered pitching a piece titled "TV: My Favorite Baby-sitter" to a parenting magazine.

To the playground, that totalitarian state of misery where children become terrorists, I wore a 1927 Yankees baseball cap with oversized Versace aviator sunglasses, like Madonna not wanting to be recognized. I couldn't stand overhearing the conversations about the sorts of things that used to be normal to me: dinners at Isabella's, going somewhere warm in January, buying something because you just had to have it. Though vastly different from the Upper East Side, where the playgrounds are filled with Hermès Birkin bags, professionally applied Clarins self-tanner, Mini Cooper–sized diamonds, creamy sorbet-colored cashmere sweaters, and Tod's loafers, the Upper West Side has its own insidious wealth, like people who own multiple vacation homes (domestic and international) and don't bat an eye at spending $25,000 for nursery-school tuition.

I felt like a fraud living there.

Violet and I would get fed up with the politics and cut out early. We'd head to Gristedes and buy Goldfish crackers in place of lobster.

One day we were on the express line at the supermarket and I was feeling particularly sorry for us. I thought how much I'd like to buy an overpriced Dora the Explorer sticker book for Violet and a big pile of glossy magazines for myself. (One of our cost-saving measures was to stop renewing our numerous periodical subscriptions.)

In front of me was a very harried young Latina woman with a small baby and a fidgety toddler. She quietly approached the cashier and asked her something.

"You can't do that at the express line!" the cashier snapped. She was clearly one of those people who get really happy when they can tell someone, "No, I can't help you."

I was just about to step in when the cashier from the next aisle, whose tag said TRACEY WILLIAMS, spun around and intervened.

"Come here, honey," she said gently, bringing the young mother over. With a big smile and an air of total discretion and respect, she left her post and retrieved a case of baby formula the young mother needed to purchase with food stamps.

Tracey took care of the whole transaction in the blink of an eye, and with words of comfort about how it would get easier when the little one slept, she sent them on their way. She wasn't a manager, just an extremely decent and kind person. I heard her tell someone else that she remembered getting up at four in the morning to leave the Bronx to come to Gristedes and getting a call from a day-care worker who said she didn't have her child's soy formula. She laughed and shook her head at the memory.

I left the store, weeping as I walked home, and sent a letter to the main office of Gristedes saying what an exemplary employee the store had. I envied Tracey and all of her life skills. I felt pretty embarrassed about the self-pity I'd been wallowing in. Not getting my hair blonded at Bergdorf's every six weeks wasn't exactly cause for a fund-raising concert: "*. . . and now Sting with an announcement for Double Process with Buttery Highlights Aid.*"

Paul and I decided to go to my parents' house for a few days to try to figure things out. Our options were putting our stuff in storage and moving in with my parents or putting our stuff in storage and moving out to Mattie's house in Montauk. I hated our options.

Up at my parents' home, Paul and I talked and thought about what we could do without, other than money. While we spoke, I sat on the floor of the living room by the antique breakfront and pulled out all the stuff in there. Grandma Pearl's and Grandpa Saul's high school diplomas, some photos from their honeymoon, and a familiar plastic bag from Dellwood Country Club in New City, New York, where my grandparents had lived for a bit before going to Florida.

It was one of those things that was always in that drawer, but I'd never bothered to go through it. The bag was cloudy clear plastic so you could see the contents: some Haggadahs, a dozen or more sterling-silver kiddush cups, and various yarmulkes. I dumped it on the floor.

Among the handful of thin, unmarked black funereal stock was a yarmulke from a 1953 trip to Israel, a tourist souvenir. The rest were the personalized type that you get at a wedding or a bar mitzvah. I started reading them aloud to Paul, explaining whom they belonged to.

A white satin that said:

WEDDING RECEPTION
IN HONOR OF
MR. & MRS. PHILIP S. GIPS
JUNE 17, 1958
ESSEX HOUSE

This was my mother's cousin Barbara.

Another white satin that said:

WEDDING RECEPTION
IN HONOR OF
MR. & MRS. STEPHEN PAUL MOSKOWITZ
SEPTEMBER 5, 1965
RIVERDALE TEMPLE

No idea who this was.

White velvet with gold swirly trim that said:

BAR MITZVAH RECEPTION OF
STUART MICHAEL WEISS
NOVEMBER 22, 1959
MONSEY PARK HOTEL

Not a clue, but a really swanky yarmulke.

A white satin that said:

WEDDING RECEPTION
IN HONOR OF
MR. & MRS. ALBERT KAHN
JUNE 22, 1965
FOUNTAINHEAD

My mother's cousin Doris.

A baby-blue satin yarmulke I recognized right away:

BAR MITZVAH RECEPTION OF
MATTHEW CHARLES KLAM
MAY 28, 1977

Another one I recognized, dark purple satin:

BAR MITZVAH
BRIAN JEFFREY KLAM
MAY 24, 1975

Paul asked me where *my* yarmulke was. I said there wasn't one because I didn't have a bat mitzvah. My mother said we all had the choice to have a bar or bat mitzvah; the boys chose to have them and I chose not to. I couldn't hack regular school. *Hebrew* school? Forget it.

I picked up another purple:

THE BAR MITZVAH OF
MICHAEL ADAM GIPS
OCTOBER 8, 1977

My mother's cousin Barbara's son.

Another white:

WEDDING RECEPTION OF
ROBIN AND MATTHEW SOLINGER
JANUARY 25, 1968
REGENCY HOTEL

My grandmother's brother Julius's son's wedding (DEE-VORCED).

A white velvet one that said:

WEDDING RECEPTION
IN HONOR OF
MR. & MRS. RONALD O. PERELMAN
JUNE 27, 1965
ESSEX HOUSE

Paul and I looked at each other. Ronald Perelman? Ellen Barkin's husband? Revlon president?

"MAAAAAAAAA," I yelled. "What the hell?"

My mother came over and looked at it. "Oh, funny," she said.

"Yeah? And?"

"My grand-uncle Sam owned the Essex House. That was his granddaughter."

For some reason, when I was a kid, I was under the impression that I was a great-grandniece of Irving Berlin. I am not. It was time for me to get the whole story. What had my grandfather meant by our being royalty? Where were the crown jewels, and could I sell them?

MY GRANDMOTHER PEARL'S PEOPLE, a mishmash of Eastern European Jewish shtetlers, emigrated from Moscow first to England, then to New York in the late nineteenth century. No one knows why they left England, but I'm guessing it was the food.

At the New York Public Library I began digging through archives to see what I could find. I had little snippets of information from my mother and aunts but none of it agreed. I felt that getting this research and putting it together to form a complete picture would somehow save my family. Release us. Something.

The week I spent delving revealed bits and pieces of my history that were astounding, mainly because they simply existed. Every day was like a trip back in time. I found my mother's grandmother, Rose, whom I was named after (my middle name is Rose) in a *New York Times* story from September 2, 1933. She was on a passenger list from the ocean liner *Dixie*. The ship had run aground on a Florida reef, leaving Rose (in first class) and the rest of the four hundred passengers stranded. She was an elegant lady, and she had no clue what to do with her high-stepping, high-maintenance flapper daughter, Pearl.

In 1926 Pearl announced she was going to college; her mother was dumbfounded by this choice. Why would a girl want to go to college? Such an independent streak was unheard of; maybe Pearl was a career-minded go-getter after all. Rose wanted her to be happy, so she gave her ten dollars to enroll at Columbia. The following day, Pearl received a stunning revelation from her friend Annie, a fact apparently everyone but Pearl knew: all the cute boys were at NYU. Pearl sobbed to her mother that she'd made a terrible mistake. So her mother gave her another ten dollars and she transferred to NYU.

Pearl told my grandfather, one of the cute NYU boys and a manager of the Happiness Candy Store, that she wasn't getting married until she was thirty. She married him in her sophomore year. They had four daughters, my mother being the third, and raised them in a modern 1930s home but trained them in Pearl's old-fashioned man-hunting techniques. The instructions were: do what you need to do to get married. If you go to college, make it business school, where the men are. If you want to learn to play tennis or piano, do it; it will make you a better and more entertaining wife.

None of that was in the *Times*, although it was there that I found out about Rose's brothers, Samuel, Simon, and Joseph Golding. (Both Samuel and Simon were called Sam.)

According to their obituaries, which were the large, featured kind with a photo, reserved for people of note, Joseph was born in 1872 in Butyan, Lithuania; Simon was born in Russia in 1883; and Samuel was born in 1886. Rose had four small paid death notices. They were from her family, the Ladies' Auxiliary of the Rabbi Jacob Joseph School, the officers and directors of the Rabbi Jacob Joseph School, and the Blue Star Circle of Riverdale. Other than the fact that she was deeply mourned and very much beloved, they contained little information and were very hard to read.

Samuel was the most distinguished, having founded the Sterling National Bank, which opened in 1929. Under his chairmanship, Sterling opened four branches, had total assets of $300 million, and became the thirteenth-largest commercial bank in New York City. Among his cited accomplishments was the fact that when President Franklin Delano Roosevelt called for a bank holiday in 1933, Sterling was one of the few banks to stay open. He was also prominent in real estate developing, along with his brothers. The Queens neighborhood of Rego Park, according to family lore, was named after my great-grandmother, ROSE GOlding. He owned the Essex House, the Regency Hotel, and the Chatham Hotel, and was part owner of Imperial House, hence the preponderance of family weddings and bar mitzvahs at Essex House and the Regency.

He was also a significant philanthropist. He'd given a million dollars to Albert Einstein Medical College to establish the Sue Golding Graduate School, named after his late wife. (His second wife was heir to the Hartz Mountain fortune—my grandmother explained this as "money finds money.") He was a substantial contributor to Beth Israel Hospital and the Lincoln Center for the Performing Arts.

Simon and Joseph were no slouches either, owning Golding Brothers Company, a hugely successful cotton goods merchant and manufacturer. Their charitable gifts supported the Joseph Golding Medical Research Fund, the Rabbi Jacob Joseph School on Henry Street, the Home for Daughters of Jacob, and the Home for Daughters of Israel.

My great-grandmother Rose married Isaac Solinger, someone who felt dissed by the Brothers Golding. He started his own company and did quite well, though not big-*New-York-Times*-obituary well.

The gleaning of this history snowballed, and soon I was getting stories from my mother and her sisters about how much Sam adored Rose and his niece, Pearl. Pearl loved him, too, but didn't like to invite him over much to her Riverdale home; she thought he'd think she was looking for money. When Sam did visit, he'd bring her little tokens of his fondness, things like a mink stole or an alligator purse. I pictured the born-again Ebenezer Scrooge visiting his nephew and his wife on Christmas Day, but in fact Uncle Sam was kind to begin with and had a family of his own, and they all celebrated Hanukkah instead of Christmas. But you get the idea.

I read more about the Goldings. While Rose lived up in Washington Heights, her brothers would all have been my neighbors on the Upper West Side. Simon lived at 250 West Ninety-fourth Street, an apartment building I always looked out onto while I was on the elliptical machine at the gym. Joseph lived at 262 Central Park West, just south of Margot.

I started thinking about the legacy of the women. There is nothing new about the notion that men historically have been more valued than women, but in my grandmother's family and my mother's family and, more subtly, in my own family, it was taken to the extreme. Girls really were treated like princesses, meant to make good marriages for their families. Mine isn't a heritage of girl babies being dumped in the river or sold to the highest bidder. Instead, we were choked with diamonds and smothered in furs.

If Rose and Pearl had been born male, they, too, would have been millionaire power brokers. It would have been their birthright. But as women they were not in line for any part of the throne; they had to rely on the kindness of their male family members, or land a big fish of their own.

But Pearl was nobody's fool. She was tough and funny and interesting. She drove a bus for the VA during the war, and was rumored to be able to fix an engine with a bobby pin. She had sayings like "I like things to get old on *me*" (why she didn't buy antiques). "It doesn't ask for food" (if you debated bringing a sweater along to dinner). Her favorite saying, though, was "If you're a bear, dance." It meant if you were taken advantage of, you asked for it. Like a dancing bear in the circus, which, I guess she felt, has the power to clobber its master instead of waltzing. If you were unhappy, change the situation, because if you didn't, then you were just a dancing bear.

She didn't always say it out loud, though. When my

mother complained about how long it took her to go down to Little Italy to buy cannoli for my father, Grandma Pearl just mimed a dancing bear, paws in the air, doing a two-step.

"All right, all right!" my mother would say.

She was content with her life, and my mother was content with her life. I was not content with my life. I needed to stop feeling like a dancing bear.

The answer to the riddle I'd been looking for was simple. By marrying Paul, I had escaped my destiny of being a rich, pampered wife. That life never would have satisfied me. There was a point in time I might have denied this, but no longer. I knew I wanted to be different.

Now I saw that the hole of my former fate needed to be filled. It was no longer just me I was responsible for, it was my legacy, my own daughter, Violet.

What is that place within yourself that doesn't exist one day and the next day is all that you are made of? It's what turns ordinary hobbits into heroes and layabouts into breadwinners. The commodity I had was an ability to write, but I'd been out of the game so long that I had no clue as to how to get back in. But I was going to figure it out.

When we were growing up, Brian was the brother who told me I was adopted, and that while I was at Amy Pollack's house my parents had revised their will to leave him all of their money. Things had changed, though, and during the bad times I was having as an adult, he was so actively solicitous, he'd call many times a day to check in on us, make suggestions, and be supportive. Whatever financial woes we had, I knew I had hit the jackpot with my family.

Brian had built a successful radio advertising company, and he knew what it felt like to knock on doors for business. He suggested talking to friends at magazines, but I didn't have any anymore. He said that his college roommate's wife was a magazine editor, and that I should pitch to her. I started waffling, but then I thought about Tracey Williams from Gristedes. I sent out a pile of pitches.

Six weeks later I heard back. The editor liked one of my pitches, the one about my ex-boyfriend the ex-convict. I got the assignment and it was going to be a big feature, and for that one story I was getting paid more than we'd made the whole previous year.

My confidence lifted, I turned into a pitching machine. I would walk around and think of everything as a magazine story. Cleaning the bathroom, I'd think, "I don't wear rubber gloves. That's interesting. I don't care about my nails—I'm a beauty junkie who eschews her nails." *ZOOM-pitch!*

I put a load into my washing machine and thought, "This apparatus has changed my life. Having a washing machine is really women's liberation." *ZOOM-pitch!*

I didn't sell every pitch, but I got work. The first milestone was that for one month we didn't need to borrow money to pay our bills. We did need to cut our monthly nut significantly, though, by moving to a cheaper apartment.

We combed the papers and spent an inordinate amount of time looking at dumps. Every few days we'd decide to quit, and then, like addicts, one of us would be back on the real estate sites or in the classifieds.

"What about Harlem? What about Bedford-Stuyvesant? What about the Rockaways? Where *are* the Rockaways?"

One morning I checked my e-mail. There was a message from Barbara, asking if you could be hypnotized to stop eating peanut-butter cups, and one from a broker we'd met, Gus. He'd just gotten a listing that had "the one" written all over it. I asked Paul if he would call and set it up. We were told to meet Gus on the corner of 150th Street and Broadway in half an hour.

We got there first and went right into our cursory check—"Is that where we'd grocery shop?" "Where would we fill prescriptions?" "Do we *need* automotive parts?"

I asked Paul if my father grew up on 155th and Broadway or 150th and Broadway. He didn't remember. When the broker arrived I was dialing my parents to find out. As we approached the building, Gus asked us to wait; he had to get keys.

My dad answered the phone, "Hello . . . *Julie!*" For some people caller ID never gets old.

"Dad, where was your apartment?" I asked.

"Hell. It was in shit-fuck-hell," he said.

My mother was on the other extension. "A Hundred and Fiftieth and Broadway."

"Really? What was the house number?"

As he spoke, I looked at the numbers.

"Five sixty-nine."

Five six nine! "Oh my God, Dad, I'm at your building!"

"Run!" he said.

"What apartment did you live in?" I asked as Gus came back out with the keys. Dad and Gus spoke at the same time.

"We'll be going to look at apartment 4A."

"We lived in 4A."

"Oh Jesus," my father said. "You can't move there. I'll have nightmares!"

"I'll call you back," I said.

We entered the building and looked at the broken, gritty tile and the dark, cascading staircase. I saw my dad being chased up the stairs—these were long flights. Paul and Violet went up in the elevator with Gus, but I wanted to walk. It was my dad's Trail of Tears.

I had chills and nausea as I went up, thinking about him being so scared and alone, and it happened every day.

When I was a kid, I would race from our kitchen through the dark dining room and living room till I got to the stairs, because I imagined I was being pursued by bears.

By the time Gus opened the door that my dad had been hunted to every day, I knew we couldn't take it; it was too sad and, mind-bogglingly, too expensive. I looked around at the renovations and went out to the fire escape to call my father back.

"I'm on your fire escape."

"Really?"

"I'm looking down Broadway and across to Riverside."

"Can you still see the park?"

"Yes, a sliver."

"We had a sliver view," he said, "instead of a river view."

I laughed. In my imagination, the apartment was in sepia tones, there was a cathedral-style radio playing *Little Orphan Annie*, and my grandparents' dark, depressing paintings covered the walls.

"It now has four bedrooms and two bathrooms."

"Oh boy, could we have used that," he said quietly. "You know, we could see some knockout sunsets there, because we faced west."

"It's not a bad place at all," I said, lying a little—it wasn't bad, but it wasn't great.

"You going to take it?" he asked hesitantly.

"No, Dad, they're charging twenty-four hundred a month." Though it was less than our current rent, it didn't pay to move.

"Fuckin' bastards," he barked. "Tell them we were paying fifty bucks a month!"

We walked home and looked for the sunset and laughed about the fact that we couldn't afford my father's famous Harlem tenement slum! We were a loser's loser.

WHEN I GRADUATED from college, I thought that facials should be covered by insurance, and here, fifteen years later, I was washing out zip-lock bags and stretching a chicken dinner into three nights of meals. I went from getting lingerie at La Petite Coquette to buying underwear at Duane Reade. I reused dryer sheets and tea bags. I mended holes in Paul's clothes instead of chucking them and buying new, and I developed a love for Kirkland, the Costco brand.

Besides Brian, there were other significant ports in our storm. Adam Resnick and I had remained close since my Letterman days, and he let me know he was there for me daily. A successful screenwriter, Adam sent Paul's script to a production company and got another producer friend interested in my magazine article to develop into a movie. In fact, so many people, friends and family, came through for us that I felt a little like George Bailey at the end of *It's a Wonderful Life*, when he discovers the inscription on the inside cover of Clarence's copy of *The Adventures of Tom Sawyer*: "Dear George, Remember NO MAN is a failure who has friends. Thanks for the wings! Love, Clarence."

It seemed like one day I turned around and was making money. I got up in the morning, brought my coffee to my computer, and, except for a million interruptions ("Excuse me, Mommy, but I think Beatrice wants you to play ponies with her"), sat writing all day. Checks came in, and, as if the universe had been waiting for me to get to a certain point before opening the gate, one day Paul got a job!

Thirteen

The Daughter Also Rises

I HAD THIS FEELING that once we braved the rough waters, life would be all good: swaying palm trees, a glittering ocean, and a winking moon. Forever and ever. The End. But that's just not how it went. In June 2005, my father's sister, Suzie, worn down by her unfair fight with ALS, died at the age of fifty-six.

Five months later, on the night before Thanksgiving, my mother's sister Phyllis, the pretty one, died of cancer. She was still beautiful.

During what Paul and I began to call our Dark Time, I kept a list in the back of my appointment book of the things I planned to do when we got money. Other than the obvious—paying off our debts and getting my hair properly colored and cut—the whole list consisted of things for Violet:

- buy Violet Petit Bateau and TSE cashmere clothes
- take Violet to the Plaza for tea; look for Eloise
- sign Violet up for fun classes (tennis? ballet?)
- buy back the jewelry I had to sell to give to Violet
- take Violet on Caribbean vacation so she can see water that isn't brown
- take Violet to FAO Schwarz to buy her a fairy-princess costume

Getting out of the Dark Time was a very long process. While I can afford things now, I wouldn't dream of spending the kind of money I used to again, though every so often I slip. Recently I bought Violet a pink tie-dyed skirt with a rhinestone heart. She loved it, so I went back to the store and got her five more of the same skirt, in green, blue, yellow, orange, and purple. I was acting like my mother, except the skirt was $5.99, not $200. No big surprise, Violet wears the pink one every day and leaves the others in her closet.

I finally realized that the best endowment I could give her is not on the list. It's profoundly intangible: self-reliance.

My mother was never the type to say, *Wait till you have kids, you'll see!* She never had any interest in making us feel guilty. But you do see when you have children that it is impossible not to make mistakes with them. I think about how much it used to drive me crazy that my mother would read instead of play dollhouse with me. I don't know if I'm doing Violet a favor or not by working from home, because I'm here, but I'm busy. She can have me, but she can't. I can make her lunch, but I can't have a pony tea party when I have a story due. Though God knows there is nothing I would like better than to spend the morning with strawberry-cab-air-freshener-scented horses with eerily long manes.

It's hard for me to let Violet struggle with the pieces of a puzzle, especially when I can see so clearly where they go. It's difficult for me to let her negotiate with the obnoxious five-year-old at the playground who is excluding her, when I could so easily put the kid in a chokehold.

On the flip side, I worry about her being in fourth-grade math class and in the throes of bubonic plague because I'm so afraid to take her out of school lest she get behind. I should just start a therapy savings account for her now.

It's something I never imagined I'd feel, but I am so grateful for what I went through, because without it I never would have found out what I am made of. And I never would have known that all of those teachers who admonished me for not applying myself were right.

The other morning, before I started working, I got an e-mail from a friend. It said:

> Hey Jul, Do you have any advice for a friend—she's having some issues with her husband who is out of work and she is going crazy because she feels upset that she is the only one working. She was raised to be a bit of a princess and married him because she thought he would be rich (he's got rich parents), so she's VERY

> disappointed. He has motivation problems and doesn't do a lot around the house (she has three girls), so it is understandably infuriating, but it is particularly hard for her because the Arabian culture/crowd is all about labels, money, showing off, etc., so she constantly looks at what she doesn't have. XO, Meg

I cut-and-pasted the line "Do you have any advice . . ."

I wrote: "Yes. Tell her not to raise her daughters to be princesses." I also wrote about my own struggles with figuring out who I was in relation to my own life and not the life of my culture. It turns out, after a lot of exploration, that I'm not really a princess. A swell gal, sure, but not a princess.

MARGOT AND I talked about how I ultimately ended up on my feet. She thought for a long time before speaking.

"Clearly, you have worked very hard," she said. "In terms of your mother—the mistakes she made did not come from a lack of care or belief in you. Her lack of support in your competence, the limited value she put on this, seemed to come from a lack of appreciation for its importance for a woman in the world and as part of your development. Not allowing you to experience discomfort came from her own way of managing her world—denying her pain and her not being able to tolerate your discomfort. She dealt with you in the best way she knew, given the constellations she was operating in—her defensive structure. The bottom line is that I think your inner core—your sense of your value and importance as a human being—remained intact. You have always known you are special and have something to offer. Your competence and creativity were simply undeveloped." She thought for a moment, then added, "You felt incompetent, but you never felt worthless. That was all your mother."

In mid-October, my friend Deirdre asked me to do a reading of a diary I wrote for the pregnancy book she co-created. It was on a Tuesday evening, and she wanted me to bring Violet along as an illustration of why it's worth it to suffer through pregnancy. All day I debated: Should I? Should I not? Violet has awful motion sickness, and the reading was downtown on the East Side, not near any trains. It started at seven p.m., right around her bedtime. In the end, all signs of sense pointed to "not such a hot idea."

Paul came home from work early and said, "What do you want to do?"

He offered to either come along with her or stay home with her, whichever I chose.

"I'm not bringing her," I said finally.

"I want to go, Mom!" Violet said, dressed casually in a tutu and crown and pink fluffy boots.

EARLIER IN THE DAY I'd told her I would be going out in the evening. Since this was a rare occurrence, she wanted to know all about it. I told her I'd be reading a story for some people. She suggested *A Kiss for Little Bear* and *Angelina Ballerina,* two most certain crowd pleasers. I told her that I'd be reading a story I made up, and she frowned and pressed *A Kiss for Little Bear* and *Angelina Ballerina* into my hands.

When she stands at the door asking to come, I break it to her that I will be reading the crummy thing I wrote—no ballerinas, no bears, no pictures.

"I want to go," she says.

"I want to go, too," Paul echoes.

We gather Violet's "friends"—a stuffed patchwork cat our friend made her named Polka, and her blanket, Gacky.

It is when the cab stops at a light at Fifty-first and Park, in front of St. Bart's Church, that I first notice Violet's face getting pale and her skin feeling clammy. These are the signals that precede my getting barfed on.

"Stop the cab, please!" I say.

We quickly kiss good-bye at Forty-sixth Street, Paul and Violet get out of the cab to walk to the subway to go home, and I continue on alone to my reading.

When I arrive, I notice that in addition to Violet's not being there, Deirdre is not there. Later I find out that two hours after her appearance promoting the book on the *Today* show, her water broke. Mother and baby girl were doing well.

Barbara is there before me, and we have just started talking about her cool new bangs when she points to the door and says, "Look who's here!"

It is Paul and Violet, smiling and pushing their way through the crowd.

"Hi, Mom," Violet says, hopping on Barbara's lap.

After the introductions, Deirdre's coauthor invites me up

to the front of the room to read. There are two seats for the two authors, and I sit in one. When I look down beside me, the other seat is occupied by Violet.

"My publicist," I mumble.

I do my reading with Violet next to me, and throughout, she looks at the audience, and then at me, and at Paul and Barbara. A few seconds after people laugh at something I read, she laughs, too, and then everyone laughs again.

At the culmination, people clap, and Violet and I go back to gather our things.

"That was great, Mom!" Violet says.

"Thanks, sweetie!" I squeeze her.

"I sat in the chair next to you," she tells me.

"I know, you sat so nicely!" I say, and ask, "Did you like the story?"

She looks at me, smiling sweetly, and says, "Next time you could read *Little Bear* and *Angelina*!"

"As soon as we get home," I say, carrying her out into the night air.

VIOLET AND MY PARENTS have an enviable relationship. Nary a thought crosses Violet's mind that doesn't inspire her to pick up the phone and call Bubbe and Papa to share. She will come into the apartment after an outing with her hand on her chin and say, "I better call Papa and tell him about my new blue balloon."

With my mother she discusses complaints about me and emotions she's feeling and what she's watching on TV and what she had for lunch. She also asks my mother if she would please go to her garage and get her car and drive it to the toy store and get Violet a new _________ (pony, paint set, sidewalk chalk, bubbles, yo-yo, etc.).

"Bubbe," Violet says to my mother over the phone, watching her own sad face in the mirror, "before when Mom said I couldn't have ice cream, I was sad, and I cried."

"Oh no!" my mother wails. "When I come down we'll have to get you a present!"

My mother comes down to visit as often as she can, and usually she, Violet, and Mattie have lunch at Saks. (And I take advantage of the free baby-sitting.)

Recently I met the three of them at the playground near our apartment after their girls' lunch out. I walked our dog, Bea, over and spotted Violet on the slide, dressed in head-to-toe pink accented with blobs of chocolate ice cream, with my mother and Mattie watching her and talking. When I approached, a little boy came running over to see Bea. Violet followed and told the boy that Bea was her dog and asked him what his name was.

"I'm Violet, this is Mom, this is Mattie, this is Bubbe, this is Bea." He ignores her and keeps petting Bea.

"Maybe he's shy," she says and repeats the entire thing again. He continues to pay her no heed.

"HEY!" Mattie shouts at him. "SHE ASKED YOU YOUR NAME. ARE YOU DEAF? WHAT'S YOUR NAME?"

The kid immediately obliges: "Maxwell Philip Schwartzman."

"Maxwell," Mattie says calmly, "this is Violet."

He keeps petting Bea as Mattie talks with him. It turns out he loves dogs and isn't allowed to have one, "even though if it pooped on the floor I'd clean it up with a wipe." Mattie, finding a kindred spirit in him, tries to help him think of a way to get a dog.

Violet then heads over to the sandbox, where my mother and I dangle our size 10 pedicures. Twin little boys are playing with some sort of sieves with handles. Violet watches them covetously.

"Can I have a net, Mom?" Violet asks.

I watch my mother's mind racing: What can she do? Should she fashion a net from a tree branch? Take the nets from these kids? She puts her camera in her purse and zips it.

"I'm going to get her one," she tells me. The toy store is ten blocks away.

"Sit down, Mom," I say to her, and to Violet, "We don't have one. There are fifty million toys in the sandbox, play with something else."

"I want a net so I can catch a whale like Little Bear."

"Why can't I get her one?" my mother pleads, still standing.

"Because she doesn't need it."

"She has to catch a whale!"

I picture my mother coming back to the playground with $10,000 in fishing equipment and an animatronic whale. The two of us go back and forth—me saying, "You don't need to get her everything she wants," my mother saying, "It's a toy net, not a Mercedes." And suddenly we see Violet: she has gone to the twins' mother and asked if she can have a turn with the net when they're through.

"Actually," the mom says, "we have another one in the stroller."

She goes to get it and gives it to Violet, while my mother and I stare, stunned. Violet plays with it for two minutes, catches a handful of whales, and returns it. Then she skips off to the swings, where she introduces herself to some older girls.

My mother and I look at each other.

"I never would've thought of that," I say with a tone approaching reverence.

"She didn't learn that from me," Mom says.

"Well, good," I say, "I'm glad she got it from somewhere."

My mother nods, thinks.

"You know," she says, looking at me intently, "I'm going to buy her a net."

I give my mother a kiss. "I know you are, Mom."

ACKNOWLEDGMENTS

EVEN BEFORE I KNEW what this book would be, I was thinking about how I could ever possibly thank Esther Newberg for all she's done for me. As anyone who knows the publishing world can tell you, Esther is respected, revered, and a little feared. What people don't know is that Esther (whom my mother calls "a looker") is the kind of person who will respond to your panicked questions at nine p.m. on a Friday night from a box in Fenway Park—and give you the score (and let you know the Yankees, wherever they are, are losing). She is the kind of person who lets my daughter, who still thinks her name is Buster, wander around her office playing with prized autographed baseballs and priceless first editions and talk and talk and talk while publishing kingpins are waiting for her on hold. I can never, ever begin to explain the depth of my gratitude and love for Esther without getting verklempt and breaking into song. God willing, there will be an audiobook.

Among Esther's too-numerous-to-name gifts is literary yenta, matching her authors with the editors of their dreams—in my case, the very brilliant Megan Lynch. Who would have thought that the valedictorian of an all-girls Catholic high school in Philadelphia would get me better than I get myself? Aside from the fact that she is sensitive, stunning, clever, chic, generous, tactful, and hilarious, she is also an expert at dealing with certain people's anxiety attacks like a human Xanax. I pray to Jesus she'll edit me for the rest of our lives. Amen.

Tremendous thanks to the Great and the Good Geoff Kloske, and to everyone at Riverhead Books, *the best darn publishing house in the business!*

And in alphabetical order, love and thanks and thanks and thanks and thanks and thanks to Sarah Bowlin, Martha Broderick, Rocket Cohen, Lillian Dean, Jancee Dunn, Christine Earle, Margaret and Patrick Fox, Jessica Green, The Group (Carol, Jackie, Jessica, Maria, Pat), Wendy Hammond, Lisa Heller, Dr. Vesna Jovanovic, Ruth Davis Konigsberg, David Letterman, Jessica Medoff, Kristin Moavenian, Michael O'Connor and Stephanie Shea O'Connor, Steve O'Donnell, Sharda Persaud, Adam Resnick, Erin Zammett Ruddy, Kari Stuart, Leslie Verbitsky, Janet Waddell, and Barbara Warnke.

Grateful acknowledgment to the Pember Library and Museum in Granville, New York.

Heaps of love to all the far reaches of my family, especially Mattie, all the brothers—John, Bob, David, Brian, and Matthew—and my magnificent parents.

And to Paul, my universe.

IN LOVING MEMORY OF

Saul Smith, Pearl Smith,

Phyllis Smith Grigor, Iris Smith Snyder